MAYWOOD PUBLIC LIBRARY

7-09

W9-BLG-003

11

# 50 High-Impact, Low-Care Garden Plants

Maywood Public Library
121 S. 5th Ave.
Maywood, IL 60153

# 50 High-Impact, Low-Care Garden Plants

TRACY DISABATO-AUST

TIMBER PRESS
PORTLAND · LONDON

Text by Tracy DiSabato-Aust.
Photography credits appear on page 168.

Copyright © 2008 by Tracy DiSabato-Aust. All rights reserved.

Published in 2008 by
Timber Press, Inc.

The Haseltine Building
133 S.W. Second Avenue, Suite 450
Portland, Oregon 97204-3527
www.timberpress.com

2 The Quadrant
135 Salusbury Road
London NW6 6RJ
www.timberpress.co.uk

Second printing 2009

Printed in China

Library of Congress Cataloging-in-Publication Data

DiSabato-Aust, Tracy.
    50 high-impact, low-care garden plants / Tracy DiSabato-Aust.
        p. cm.
    Includes bibliographical references.
    ISBN-13: 978-0-88192-950-8
 1. Plants, Ornamental.  2. Low maintenance gardening.  3. Companion planting.
 I. Title.  II. Title: Fifty high-impact, low-care garden plants.
    SB404.9.D57 2009
    635.9–dc22
                            2008010676

A catalog record for this book is also available from the British Library.

In loving memory of my father,
Louis DiSabato, whose wide smile,
contagious laughter, and passion
for life will always dance
in his baby girl's heart.

# Contents

# Introduction

Iwrote this book because you might be like me. You love to garden, but there is never enough time. You know you should study those lists of "low-maintenance" plants in the garden magazines, but you don't want to sacrifice excitement just for the sake of easy care.

Life is hectic. In an effort to achieve that elusive life balance, we inevitably give up something we love to do—if you're reading this book, then that something might be gardening. If so, you're also giving up just the thing you need to help manage your stress-filled, hectic life.

So where do plants fit into all of this? Plants can be a tonic for the soul, rejuvenating the spirit. They can serve as a grounding connection to nature—something that is so needed by all of us in this frantic Bluetooth, BlackBerry, iPod nano, big-screen world. But plants shouldn't add to our stress by being demanding and difficult. We should be able to enjoy them without being enslaved by them.

I've been a gardener for over thirty years both as an avocation and vocation. I love gardening but I also have countless other passions including spending time with my husband, our teenage son, and our dogs and chickens, as well as being a competitive multisport athlete (triathlon/duathlon) at the national and international level. So I'm constantly rethinking areas of my garden and seeking beautiful yet tough plants to replace demanding ones. I refer to them affectionately as indomitable—not easily defeated, resolute, unconquerable, determined, and strong. Does this sound like the type of plant for you?

These plants should not only be easy to care for but they should bring passion and excitement into our lives with their colors, textures, shapes, and scents. It's great if a plant is easy to grow, but if it's of minimal ornamental value, who really cares? With plants, like all things in our lives, we want to have our cake and eat it too. We want beautiful, wonderful things but we don't want to devote countless hours to them because we don't have countless hours. Hence, the premise for this book.

*50 High-Impact, Low-Care Plants* was inspired by an article I wrote for *Fine Gardening* magazine in 2005 titled "High-Impact, Low-Care Plants: The Best Showstoppers are the Ones That Don't Need Pampering." The topic was so well received that I felt it should be expanded into a book. Whether you are a newbie to gardening or a seasoned veteran, this book was written for you and your busy life. I want you to enjoy the pleasure of plants and gardening no matter what's on your Day-Timer. And if you are a professional in the industry these selections will give you artistic, superior choices for your clients' gardens that they'll actually be able to grow.

I selected these 50 plants based on what I consider to be a highly ornamental plant that requires minimal care. It's not all-inclusive and I'm sure you may have some favorites of your own to add to the list. These plants aren't perfect (but few things are), and some are as close to ideal as we are going to get while still working with living things. Some of my choices have more issues than others, but if I felt they provided so much beauty and pleasure that a touch of coddling was acceptable, they made the cut. After all, we don't want to completely give up gardening and all the benefits we reap from it. Because many of these plants are drought-tolerant and don't require heavy, if any, fertilizing to prosper, they are not only beautiful but functional and environmentally sound.

Many of the plants selected for this book are either U.S. natives, so they are adapted to our conditions, or they are award winners from around the world. They may have received top merits from notable organizations such as the Perennial Plant Association, which annually picks a Perennial Plant of the Year, or from the Royal Horticultural Society (RHS) in Wisley, England, which selects plants for their Awards of Garden Merit. These groups are usually composed of top-notch plants people who know their stuff. Validation from them is top shelf!

Plants can create living art. Here, a grouping of high-impact, low-care plants creates a cozy spot near a bench in our garden. From left, purple snakeroot, 'Sum and Substance' hosta, 'All Gold' Hakone grass, and wild-oat.

What makes a plant high impact? It should make a statement in multiple seasons because of its long-lasting bloom, its color, texture, form, or even fragrance. Better yet, it should possess all or most of these characteristics. On top of that it would be nice if it was somewhat theatrical and had a flair for the dramatic.

So first and foremost, a plant considered high impact needs to provide interest in several if not all seasons. For example, a multiseason plant may have beautiful flowers in the spring followed by foliage that has an interesting texture in the summer and then goes out with a bang of gorgeous autumn color.

Color can be provided by long-lasting flowers, or, as with most of the plants discussed in this book, by striking foliage, bark, or fruit. There are several plants among the 50 selected because of their yellow foliage. Yellow is a dominant color, acting like a magnet for the eyes—think about the draw of a candle flame. Many plants were chosen for their interesting and unusual texture or for their architectural forms, which create living art in the garden. If we rely on plants in our gardens that provide a demanding architectural presence and outstanding texture and foliage, we can keep the integrity of the design together without as much care as if we rely on plants which solely provide fleeting flowers.

All right, so it's not enough for a plant to just be dynamic—it must also be easy to grow. I like to choose my battles when it comes to maintenance, so I consider the specific chores a plant requires. For example, I'm more tolerant of plants that need pruning to look their best than I am of ones that demand frequent division or can be affected by pests. You should consider what does and does not work for you.

Over the years I've developed a two-part checklist to help me determine the pros and cons of a given plant. Each of my 50 meets most if not all five traits on the High-Impact Traits checklist. However, a plant also had to possess at least nine of the twelve traits (or about three-quarters of them) on the Low-Maintenance Traits checklist to be included in the top 50. The checklist is included with each plant entry; where the text is faded and not checked off, the plant did not meet the criteria for that particular trait.

### High-Impact Traits:

✔ MULTISEASON INTEREST

✔ COLORFUL FOLIAGE

✔ LONG-LASTING BLOOM

✔ OUTSTANDING TEXTURE

✔ ARCHITECTURAL FORM

### Low-Maintenance Traits:

✔ LONG-LIVED

✔ TOLERATES HEAT AND HUMIDITY

✔ COLD-HARDY

✔ DEER-RESISTANT

✔ RESISTANT TO INSECTS AND DISEASE

✔ REQUIRES MINIMAL OR NO DEADHEADING

✔ PROSPERS WITHOUT HEAVY FERTILIZING

✔ DOESN'T REQUIRE STAKING

✔ INFREQUENT OR NO DIVISION REQUIRED FOR FOUR OR MORE YEARS

✔ INFREQUENT OR NO PRUNING REQUIRED TO MAINTAIN DECENT HABIT, APPEARANCE, OR BEST FLOWERING

✔ NON-INVASIVE

✔ DROUGHT-TOLERANT

Remember: a plant that thrives and behaves well in some situations might sulk or get rambunctious in others, so lists of low-maintenance plants can vary a bit from region to region. The best way to reduce garden maintenance is to do some research before planting. As always, the right plant in the right place keeps care to a minimum. Be sure you know your site and climate. Determine your soil conditions, light patterns, minimum and maximum temperatures, available moisture, prevailing winds, and microclimates. In general plants prefer moist, high-organic, but well-draining soil, as well as protection from hot afternoon sun—and these plants are no exception. Most of the plants discussed here will tolerate less-than-favorable conditions, however, which is why they were selected for this book.

Resist what is known as "zonal denial," a phrase coined by renowned plantsman Sean Hogan: the urge to grow plants that are not hardy in your area. Also be aware of plants that may be invasive in your region by consulting the Internet or your county extension agent.

Life is short. Go for the gusto, keep it simple, and have fun with these 50 stunning, high-impact, indomitable plants.

# *Abies lasiocarpa* var. *arizonica* 'Compacta'
# Dwarf Rocky Mountain fir

**Tracy's Notes:**

THE PLANT
*Dwarf tree; pale bluish green needles; soft texture*

HARDINESS
*Zones 5–6*

HEIGHT AND SPREAD
*10–15 ft. × 6–10 ft.*

SUN AND SHADE NEEDS
*Sun to part shade*

COMBINES WELL WITH
*Golden hops, 'Cosmopolitan' miscathus, Siberian iris*

*"The strong shape and appealing foliage color make it an impressive companion."*

This is by far my favorite conifer. It is almost a perfect pyramid, with a soft texture and gorgeous blue foliage. It always looks fantastic and with next-to-no care. What else could one ask for?

Also known as dwarf corkbark fir, this beautiful, intermediate-size conifer is slow-growing at first and normally reaches only about 10 to 15 ft. in height and 6 to 10 ft. in width in ten years. It provides a wonderful sense of scale and proportion without pruning. I use it to add year-round interest among perennials and shrubs in one of my large mixed borders, but it would make a great specimen plant for a condominium or rooftop garden as well.

The strong shape and appealing foliage color of dwarf Rocky Mountain fir make it an impressive companion. It combines exquisitely with just about anything and I've particularly enjoyed it in association with golden hops (*Humulus lupulus* 'Bianca').

Because of its slow growth it's best to buy a decent-size plant at the start if you can find one. It is a touch unusual, so it may take some detective work to locate a good specimen. Dwarf Rocky Mountain fir eventually takes on a dense conical form with soft blue-green needles in the spring maturing to silver-blue. The bark is

The scale of *Abies lasiocarpa* 'Compacta' is reasonable—it normally reaches only 10 to 15 ft. in height and 6 to 10 ft. in width in ten years—so it won't overpower other plants.

grayish, and as the common name implies, a bit corky; better than a bit quirky I suppose! It retains its lower branches unless it's crowded by plants at its base.

Although it prefers cool locations, it has thrived for seven years in a sunny corner of my Midwest garden with a layer of mulch 2 to 3 in. deep to help keep its roots cool. This plant is a sheer delight!

### Dwarf Rocky Mountain fir low-maintenance checklist:

✔ LONG-LIVED

✔ TOLERATES HEAT AND HUMIDITY

✔ COLD-HARDY

DEER-RESISTANT

✔ INSECT AND DISEASE RESISTANT

✔ MINIMAL OR NO DEADHEADING

✔ MINIMAL OR NO FERTILIZING

✔ NO STAKING

✔ MINIMAL OR NO DIVISION

✔ MINIMAL OR NO PRUNING

✔ NON-INVASIVE

DROUGHT-TOLERANT

## *Acanthus spinosus*
# Spiny bear's breeches

Have you been seeking a bold architectural plant that makes a statement in sun or part shade? Then *Acanthus spinosus* is for you. Sporting tall substantial spikes of mauve and white snapdragon-like flowers atop shiny thistlelike leaves, this plant is a real conversation piece. Its big size, 2 to 4 ft. tall by 3 ft. wide, ensures its presence even in the largest of spaces.

And don't let its thistlelike leaves put you off, as they add amazing shape and textural variety often needed in many "ho-hum" shade designs. In fact the leaves are so incredible that they were the model of the Corinthian leaf motif used as decoration in ancient Roman and Greek architecture.

Spiny bear's breeches' spent flower heads remain attractive for several weeks after flowering has finished, giving this perennial what seems to be a very extensive flowering period. No deadheading is normally required until late summer when the deadheads finally decline. At this time there may be a few dead or tattered leaves which may be cut back (while wearing gloves!) to clean foliage. This foliage may remain evergreen or semi-evergreen depending on the severity of the winter.

In hot areas spiny bear's breeches benefits from protection from afternoon sun. Plants can

### Tracy's Notes:

**THE PLANT**
*Perennial; spikes of mauve flowers blooming June–July; shiny thistlelike leaves*

**HARDINESS**
*Zones 5–10*

**HEIGHT AND SPREAD**
*2–4 ft. × 3 ft.*

**SUN AND SHADE NEEDS**
*Sun to part shade*

**COMBINES WELL WITH**
*Drumstick onion, purple toadflax, and 'Victor Reiter Jr.' meadow cranesbill*

*"The leaves add amazing shape and textural variety often needed in many 'ho-hum' shade designs."*

spread aggressively by creeping rootstock in light soils and spreading roots are difficult to remove completely, so in that situation it's best to find a place where you are sure you want it before planting it. However, spreading is not normally a problem in clay soils.

Add *Acanthus spinosus* to your garden and give your friends something fantastic to remember when they leave.

## Spiny bear's breeches low-maintenance checklist:

✔ LONG-LIVED

✔ TOLERATES HEAT AND HUMIDITY

✔ COLD-HARDY

✔ DEER-RESISTANT

✔ INSECT AND DISEASE RESISTANT

✔ MINIMAL OR NO DEADHEADING

✔ MINIMAL OR NO FERTILIZING

✔ NO STAKING

✔ MINIMAL OR NO DIVISION

✔ MINIMAL OR NO PRUNING

✔ NON-INVASIVE

DROUGHT-TOLERANT

Spiny bear's britches' substantial height and width guarantee its prominence even in large spaces.

The flower spikes of *Acanthus spinosus* provide an unforgettable backdrop.

The mauve and white snapdragon-like flowers of *Acanthus spinosus* tend to like more sun, but they also stand up and shine in a more shaded design.

## *Acer griseum*
# Paperbark maple

**Tracy's Notes:**

THE PLANT
*Tree; cinnamon-colored exfoliating bark; red autumn leaves*

HARDINESS
*Zones 5–7(8)*

HEIGHT AND SPREAD
*18–20 ft. × 10–15 ft.*

SUN AND SHADE NEEDS
*Sun to part shade*

COMBINES WELL WITH
*Tiger lily, autumn flame miscanthus, and 'Jindai' tatarian aster*

*"I'm always awed by its beauty, and I can never resist the urge to touch its cinnamon-colored exfoliating bark."*

My love affair with *Acer griseum* began during my undergraduate studies at Ohio State University during the 1980s. I was so taken with a paperbark maple at the campus's Chadwick Arboretum that since then I've sought out this tree wherever I travel. I have two in my Ohio garden and think every garden should have at least one.

I'm always awed by its beauty, and I can never resist the urge to touch its cinnamon-colored exfoliating bark. A paperbark maple works in the landscape especially well where its bark can be backlit by the sun, but really I've never seen one that's not irresistible no matter what the lighting. It combines particularly nicely with warm-colored plants such as the flowers of tiger lily (*Lilium lancifolium* var. *splendens*) or the fall foliage of autumn flame miscanthus (*Miscanthus* 'Purpurescens'). It's a noble feature in small as well as large gardens.

Several factors make it my number-one small specimen tree: its striking bark and outstanding autumn color, its compact size (usually reaches a height of no more than 20 ft.), its adaptability to clay soils, varying pH levels, light conditions ranging from partial shade to full sun, moderate drought and salt tolerance, and no pests. Add that it basically requires no care and we have a winner!

It is difficult to resist touching paperback maple's cinnamon-colored exfoliating branches.

The outstanding autumn color of *Acer griseum* foliage brightens even the most subdued fall garden.

These plants are expensive, so take your time to pick out a nicely shaped plant, and be prepared to pay a fair amount for a small tree. But trust me, your investment will be well worth it.

Start a love affair that is guaranteed to last—plant a paperbark maple.

## Paperbark Maple low-maintenance checklist:

✔ LONG-LIVED

✔ TOLERATES HEAT AND HUMIDITY

✔ COLD-HARDY

✔ DEER-RESISTANT

✔ INSECT AND DISEASE RESISTANT

✔ MINIMAL OR NO DEADHEADING

✔ MINIMAL OR NO FERTILIZING

✔ NO STAKING

✔ MINIMAL OR NO DIVISION

✔ MINIMAL OR NO PRUNING

✔ NON-INVASIVE

✔ DROUGHT-TOLERANT

# *Acer japonicum* 'Aconitifolium'
# Fernleaf fullmoon maple

When the legendary plantsman Michael Dirr lists a plant as being "one of the most beautiful of all fall coloring shrubs" (*Manual of Woody Landscape Plants*, Stipes 1998), and when it's further backed by an Award of Garden Merit from the Royal Horticultural Society (and on a more local note selected by the Ohio Plant Selection Committee), you know to take notice!

*Acer japonicum* 'Aconitifolium' first caught my fancy when I was working as a gardener at Knightshayes Court in Devon, England, during the 1980s, and I've had a deep respect and admiration for this rare plant ever since. On the initial observation I thought it was a Japanese maple (*Acer palmatum*) of some kind, and although it closely resembles that species, it is reputedly more cold-hardy than Japanese maples as well as other fullmoon maples.

Fernleaf fullmoon maple has large deeply cut leaves which are an exotic textural addition to mixed gardens in full sun or part shade. It is very effective when used as a specimen in an intimate patio or rooftop garden, as a container plant, and wonderful, of course, in Japanese gardens. The leaves turn a fantastic brilliant red in the autumn with some inner foliage being a mix of red, orange, and yellow. For a phenomenal display I've combined it with dwarf yellow bamboo

## Tracy's Notes:

**THE PLANT**
*Shrub/small tree; red fruit, and reddish flowers blooming in April; autumn mix of red, orange, and yellow leaves*

**HARDINESS**
*Zones 5–7*

**HEIGHT AND SPREAD**
*8–10 ft. × 10 ft.*

**SUN AND SHADE NEEDS**
*Part shade*

**COMBINES WELL WITH**
*Dwarf yellow bamboo, golden-variegated sweet flag, and 'All Gold' Hakone grass*

*"Perhaps it's time to heed the advice of some of the top plant experts and bring fernleaf fullmoon maple into your world."*

(*Pleioblastus viridistriatus* 'Chrysophyllus'), which is not a low-maintenance plant. Newer branches are prominent red in the winter. Reddish ½-in. diameter flowers are subtly attractive as are the red wings on the enduring fruit.

Although the plant at Knightshayes was tree form, and about 15 ft. tall, most plants sold in nurseries are shrublike, slowly reaching about 8 to 10 ft. by 10 ft. Some dieback can occur from late spring frosts but plants recover nicely.

Perhaps it's time to heed the advice of some of the top plant experts and bring fernleaf fullmoon maple into your world.

The inner foliage of fernleaf fullmoon maple shines through its brilliant red mantle.

## Fernleaf fullmoon maple low-maintenance checklist:

✔ LONG-LIVED

✔ TOLERATES HEAT AND HUMIDITY

✔ COLD-HARDY

✔ DEER-RESISTANT

✔ INSECT AND DISEASE RESISTANT

✔ MINIMAL OR NO DEADHEADING

✔ MINIMAL OR NO FERTILIZING

✔ NO STAKING

✔ MINIMAL OR NO DIVISION

✔ MINIMAL OR NO PRUNING

✔ NON-INVASIVE

　　DROUGHT-TOLERANT

*Acer japonicum* 'Aconitifolium' dazzles with its symphony of red, orange, and yellow foliage.

## Acorus gramineus 'Ogon'
# Golden variegated sweet flag

**Tracy's Notes:**

**THE PLANT**
Perennial; fine-textured gold-yellow and green foliage

**HARDINESS**
Zones (5)6–8

**HEIGHT AND SPREAD**
10–12 in. × 12 in.

**SUN AND SHADE NEEDS**
Sun to part shade

**COMBINES WELL WITH**
Forget-me-nots, cypress spurge, and 'Plum Pudding' coral bells

*"Plants are evergreen so they also look amazing in the garden over the winter"*

This plant gets its common name "sweet flag" due to its lightly fragrant leaves, but I think the plant is "sweeet" (as the kids say) for its golden yellow and green foliage color, fine texture, compact size, and versatility in design. *Acorus gramineus* 'Ogon' works in innumerable combinations in the garden, woodland, and water's edge, or in containers inside or out!

I love the yellow and blue complementary color scheme in the spring of 'Ogon' with forget-me-nots (*Myosotis scorpiodes* 'Sapphire'). And for years now I've enjoyed it as a specimen in a cobalt-blue wall pot. It hangs outside on our house during the summer and spends the winter in our conservatory where it works as a low-maintenance house plant. Plants are evergreen so they also look amazing in the garden over the winter too. I've also delighted in the play of forms and textures which occurs between sweet flag and cypress spurge (*Euphorbia cyparissias* 'Fens Ruby').

Golden variegated sweet flag has some fantastic relatives which are also dreams to use to create striking design combinations. *Acorus gramineus* 'Oborozuki' looks very similar to *A. gramineus* 'Ogon' except the foliage appears more yellow, it's more robust, and it grows slightly taller, more upright, and less fanlike. I've inter-

Fall and winter gardens stay vibrant with the evergreen foliage of golden variegated sweet flag.

A close-up view of 'Ogon' sweet flag reveals often overlooked—but interesting—yellow inflorescences.

planted blue globe onion (*Allium caeruleum*) with it for a pleasing summer combination. *Acorus gramineus* 'Variegatus' is classy and clean looking with its white and green foliage and works beautifully mass-planted in light shade.

Enjoy these "sweeet" easy-care plants in your combinations, between stepping stones to add fragrance to your stroll, in a moist woodland as a slow spreading naturalizer, as an edger for your water garden, or as focal points in your borders and containers.

### Golden variegated sweet flag low-maintenance checklist:

✔ LONG-LIVED

✔ TOLERATES HEAT AND HUMIDITY

✔ COLD-HARDY

✔ DEER-RESISTANT

✔ INSECT AND DISEASE RESISTANT

✔ MINIMAL OR NO DEADHEADING

✔ MINIMAL OR NO FERTILIZING

✔ NO STAKING

✔ MINIMAL OR NO DIVISION

✔ MINIMAL OR NO PRUNING

✔ NON-INVASIVE

DROUGHT-TOLERANT

## *Actaea simplex* Atropurpurea Group
# Purple snakeroot

What a delight it is to have a heady fragrance penetrating the air in the garden during the late summer to early autumn, just when one is starting to tire of the whole affair. Even after years of growing plants in the *Actaea simplex* Atropurpurea Group (its synonym is *Cimicifuga ramosa* 'Atropurpurea'), they still sneak up on me as an unexpected but uplifting surprise when they start to flower. "Where is that wonderful smell coming from?" is the question I often have or hear.

Purple snakeroot has striking 18- to 24-in. ivory bottlebrush-like flower spikes that often arch down at the tip. They rise above the three-lobed purple-tinged foliage on tall thin stems which may bend toward the light when grown in dappled or even partial shade. My plant that receives early morning sun always leans toward it. Plants are stately and reach 4 to 6 ft., making them useful as a single vertical specimen in mixed-shade gardens or breathtaking as a group in woodland or natural areas. The flowers really pop if designed in front of a dark hedge or wall. And the bronze-purple foliage is enlivened in association with yellow-foliaged plants such as *Hosta* 'Sum and Substance'.

Purple snakeroot prefers rich, high-organic, moist soil in part to full shade but tolerates

**Tracy's Notes:**

**THE PLANT**
*Perennial; fragrant ivory bottlebrush-like flower spikes blooming August–September; bronze-purple foliage*

**HARDINESS**
*Zones 3–8*

**HEIGHT AND SPREAD**
*4–6 ft. × 2–4 ft.*

**SUN AND SHADE NEEDS**
*Part shade*

**COMBINES WELL WITH**
*'Sum and Substance' hosta, golden-variegated Hakone grass, and 'Jack Frost' Siberian bugloss*

*"The flowers really pop if designed in front of a dark hedge or wall."*

average mid-moisture sites. The tips of the foliage will scorch if grown in too much sun or dry soil—this isn't a huge drama, however, and I have survived it every year. Removal of a few dead leaves throughout the season and possibly supporting the leaning stems, if needed, are part of the minimal required maintenance. The flowers are followed by attractive seed capsules that remain into winter on strong stems, so don't deadhead. Foliage is toxic if eaten—so don't do that either! Two outstanding cultivars to look for are 'Brunette' and 'Hillside Black Beauty'.

## Purple snakeroot
## low-maintenance checklist:

✔ LONG-LIVED

✔ TOLERATES HEAT AND HUMIDITY

✔ COLD-HARDY

✔ DEER-RESISTANT

✔ INSECT AND DISEASE RESISTANT

✔ MINIMAL OR NO DEADHEADING

✔ MINIMAL OR NO FERTILIZING

✔ NO STAKING

✔ MINIMAL OR NO DIVISION

✔ MINIMAL OR NO PRUNING

✔ NON-INVASIVE

DROUGHT-TOLERANT

The seed capsules of purple snakeroot are eye-catching and persist into winter.

One outstanding cultivar to look for at your favorite nursery is *Actaea simplex* 'Brunette'.

The bronze-purple foliage and ivory bottlebrush-like flower spikes of *Actaea simplex* Atropurpurea Group are breathtaking in woodland or natural areas.

*Agastache* 'Blue Fortune'
# 'Blue Fortune' anise hyssop

### Tracy's Notes:

**THE PLANT**
*Perennial; lavender-blue flowers blooming July–September; aromatic foliage*

**HARDINESS**
*Zones 5–10*

**HEIGHT AND SPREAD**
*3–4 ft. × 2–3 ft.*

**SUN AND SHADE NEEDS**
*Sun to part shade*

**COMBINES WELL WITH**
*Russian sage, 'Summer Blues' delphinium, and 'Moonbeam' threadleaf coreopsis*

*"The lavender-blue flowers are harmonious with other blue or violet flowers and complement pale yellows beautifully."*

I like to think of *Agastache* 'Blue Fortune' as a plant "fit for a president"! I had been growing and designing with 'Blue Fortune' for several years and thought it was a great plant, but the deal was sealed one autumn day when I had to plant an "instant garden" for a client that would be hosting a U.S. president and 1500 of his "closest" friends. The garden was rather dull and lifeless and this was a temporary fix for the event until we could actually design the garden correctly.

Pots full of 'Blue Fortune' looked amazing with their lavender-blue bottlebrush-like flowers blooming with abandon atop 3-ft. stems. We planted them in a drift of 11 plants combined with Russian sage (*Perovskia atriplicifolia*) and *Delphinium grandiflorum* 'Summer Blues'. Before we even finished planting the rest of the border, the garden had come to life with butterflies, hummingbirds, and bees swarming the 'Blue Fortune'. And these plants continued to look fantastic until mid-November.

'Blue Fortune' is long-flowering from mid-summer into autumn with no deadheading. It is drought- and heat-tolerant. It resents wet feet, although in my experience it tolerates clay soils well. There are no pests and the aromatic leaves, smelling of black licorice when crushed, make

*Agastache* 'Blue Fortune' is well-behaved standing upright in full sun locations without staking, and plants can be left up for winter interest.

the plant deer-resistant. It is clump-forming, requires infrequent division, and is well-behaved standing upright in full sun locations without staking. The lavender-blue flowers are harmonious with other blue or violet flowers and complement pale yellows beautifully. Plants can be left up for winter interest and cut down in the spring. This plant has it going on!

## 'Blue Fortune' anise hyssop low-maintenance checklist:

✔ LONG-LIVED

✔ TOLERATES HEAT AND HUMIDITY

✔ COLD-HARDY

✔ DEER-RESISTANT

✔ INSECT AND DISEASE RESISTANT

✔ MINIMAL OR NO DEADHEADING

✔ MINIMAL OR NO FERTILIZING

✔ NO STAKING

✔ MINIMAL OR NO DIVISION

✔ MINIMAL OR NO PRUNING

✔ NON-INVASIVE

✔ DROUGHT-TOLERANT

## *Allium schubertii*
# Tumbleweed onion

Gardening is meant to be fun, and this crazy and entertaining plant will add fireworks to your garden, ignite your life, and remind you to "lighten up." As the eternal extrovert, *Allium schubertii* functions as an eye-catching, dominant element in design, but its real impact is as a splashy fashion statement—a good example of form before function.

The amusing, delectable, and massive (10 to 12 in.) violet-rose spidery flower heads appear in late spring to early summer and are borne on squatty, self-supportive 18-in. stems. As if the flowers weren't enough, they are followed by equally incredible seedheads that dry on the plant. These will remain firmly attached for months. The stems loosen from the ground just at the time unsightly holes are developing in other areas of the late summer garden. I usually lift them from their existing spot and set them into the hole as if they had grown there, thus filling out the border again. Spray painting the seedheads can add an entirely new dimension to these theatrics!

Tumbleweed onions are deer- and rodent-resistant but they can rot over the winter in heavy, poorly drained clay soils. They are usually recommended for zone 7 gardens, but I use them as short-lived bulbs in my zone 5 garden,

**Tracy's Notes:**

**THE PLANT**
*Hardy bulb; massive violet-rose, spidery flowers blooming in June, followed by attractive seedheads*

**HARDINESS**
*Zones (6)7–9*

**HEIGHT**
*18 in. × 10 in.*

**SUN AND SHADE NEEDS**
*Sun*

**COMBINES WELL WITH**
*'Blue Sapphire' perennial flax, 'Bath's Pink' dianthus, and 'Angels Choir' corn poppy*

*"Many of the alliums are sensational low-care additions to mixed gardens, so give them a try."*

happily replanting them every few years in the autumn in groups of three or five…because they are worth it! Leaves will decline upon flowering of the bulbs but are easily removed.

*Allium cristophii* (star of Persia) closely resembles *A. schubertii* except the flowers are slightly smaller and can be blended a bit more easily into combinations. Many of the alliums are sensational low-care additions to mixed gardens so give them a try. But always save room for the "gobsmacking" tumbleweed onion that can lift your spirits even on the worst of days.

## Tumbleweed onion low-maintenance checklist:

LONG-LIVED

✔ TOLERATES HEAT AND HUMIDITY

✔ COLD-HARDY

✔ DEER-RESISTANT

✔ INSECT AND DISEASE RESISTANT

✔ MINIMAL OR NO DEADHEADING

✔ MINIMAL OR NO FERTILIZING

✔ NO STAKING

✔ MINIMAL OR NO DIVISION

✔ MINIMAL OR NO PRUNING

✔ NON-INVASIVE

✔ DROUGHT-TOLERANT

The massive violet-rose spidery flower heads of tumbleweed onion combine beautifully with dianthus.

Eye-catching seedheads of *Allium schubertii* dry on the plant and remain for months, perched here atop *Geranium* Rozanne.

The star-shaped flower spheres of *Allium schubertii* are like fireworks—except safer and longer-lasting—in your garden.

# *Amsonia hubrichtii*
# Arkansas amsonia

**Tracy's Notes:**

**THE PLANT**
*Perennial; very pale light blue, star-shaped flowers blooming May– June; mid-green, threadlike leaves clear yellow in autumn*

**HARDINESS**
*Zones 3–9*

**HEIGHT AND SPREAD**
*2–3 ft. × 3 ft.*

**SUN AND SHADE NEEDS**
*Sun to part shade*

**COMBINES WELL WITH**
*Japanese anemone, 'Black Jack' sedum, 'Dallas Blues' switchgrass, 'Blue Billow' hydrangea, Virginia sweet spire, or smooth witherod viburnum*

*"Its key selling point is the gorgeous clear yellow autumn color it develops which is a vision when backlit."*

*Amsonia hubrichtii* is one of those impressive, underappreciated workhorse plants you can't believe isn't being used more in gardens. I hope you will fall in love with it, run out and buy it, and give it the credit it deserves.

This plant is a textural dream. It forms fluffy, billowy 2- to 3-ft. mounds of mid-green, linear, threadlike leaves spaced densely on the stems like bottlebrushes. It has pretty, light-blue-almost-white star-shaped flowers that are attractive at close inspection and appear after the first flush of growth. Its key selling point, however, is the gorgeous clear yellow autumn color it develops which is a vision when backlit.

This plant can be used effectively as a specimen or *en masse* with autumn-flowering plants such as Japanese anemone (*Anemone ×hybrida*) and 'Black Jack' sedum. I've particularly enjoyed it as a color complement to 'Dallas Blues' switchgrass (*Panicum virgatum* 'Dallas Blues'). It's a remarkable color and textural complement to other plants sporting outstanding autumn foliage color such as 'Blue Billow' hydrangea (*Hydrangea serrata* 'Blue Billow'), Virginia sweet spire (*Itea virginica*), or smooth witherod viburnum (*Viburnum nudum*).

This Arkansas and Oklahoma mountain native is cold-, heat-, and drought-tolerant and adapt-

Arkansas amsonia is a vision of clear yellow color when backlit in autumn, and a splendid complement to other plants in your fall garden.

able to a wide range of soils. Its flowers are a good nectar source and its foliage contains a milky sap which is unpleasant to deer. It's a reliable performer that doesn't spread but may reseed lightly. Grows best in full sun but tolerates light shade. Too much shade or wet soil may cause plants to open up. I shape and shear plants back by 4 to 6 in. after flowering to create more compact non-flopping plants, even on plants grown in full sun. I have gotten reports from some gardeners who have experienced an allergic skin reaction to the sap after pruning the plants. Gloves and long sleeves may be in order.

Add this resilient, gorgeous plant to your garden and spread the word about all its attributes.

## Arkansas amsonia low-maintenance checklist:

✔ LONG-LIVED

✔ TOLERATES HEAT AND HUMIDITY

✔ COLD-HARDY

✔ DEER-RESISTANT

✔ INSECT AND DISEASE RESISTANT

✔ MINIMAL OR NO DEADHEADING

✔ MINIMAL OR NO FERTILIZING

✔ NO STAKING

✔ MINIMAL OR NO DIVISION

✔ MINIMAL OR NO PRUNING

✔ NON-INVASIVE

✔ DROUGHT-TOLERANT

## *Angelica gigas*
# Korean angelica

My passion for *Angelica gigas* was first ignited at a lecture by the internationally acclaimed garden designer and horticulturist Piet Oudolf. A few years later, while visiting Bury Court Garden in Surrey, England, I saw his use of the plant in a border design—that is when I began drooling over this beauty and I haven't stopped since.

Korean angelica is a big, bold, stunning architectural plant that adds structure to a garden but requires minimal care. It's a designer's dream with luscious red-purple flowers and purple-tinged petioles. It grows 2 to 3 ft. wide and its self-supportive flowering stems can reach 3 to 6 ft. tall. It adds often-needed weight and depth to a border due to its color, size, and form.

It's an amazing focal point, stopping traffic when planted in groupings of seven to eleven plants in larger garden settings. Even with its size it's a great mid- to front-of-the-border "see through" plant due to the tall, relatively leafless flowering stems anchored by the massive foliage at the base. Korean angelica is biennial, blooming during the plant's second year in July and August, followed by striking seedheads. Plants may seed with abundance. The flowers attract beneficial insects and bees.

Korean angelica is awesome harmonized with

**Tracy's Notes:**

THE PLANT
*Biennial; red-purple flowers blooming July–August; purple-tinged petioles; self-supportive flowering stems*

HARDINESS
*Zones 4–8*

HEIGHT AND SPREAD
*3–6 ft. × 2–3 ft.*

SUN AND SHADE NEEDS
*Sun to part shade*

COMBINES WELL WITH
*'Gateway' Joe Pye weed, tropical smoketree, 'Eva Cullum' phlox, and 'Malepartus' maiden grass*

*"It's a designer's dream with luscious red-purple flowers and purple-tinged petioles."*

'Gateway' Joe Pye weed (*Eupatorium maculatum* 'Gateway'), tropical smoketree (*Euphorbia cotinifolia*), and 'Eva Cullum' phlox (*Phlox paniculata* 'Eva Cullum'). It's also gorgeous with ornamental grasses, particularly 'Malepartus' maiden grass (*Miscanthus sinensis* 'Malepartus'), whose inflorescences share a similar hue.

Plants prefer moist, fertile soil and full sun with afternoon shade in hot climates. Even though plants may need to be replaced every couple of years, *Angelica gigas* is worth growing for its high impact and minimal care. It will have you drooling too!

## Korean angelica low-maintenance checklist:

LONG-LIVED

✔ TOLERATES HEAT AND HUMIDITY

✔ COLD-HARDY

✔ DEER-RESISTANT

✔ INSECT AND DISEASE RESISTANT

✔ MINIMAL OR NO DEADHEADING

✔ MINIMAL OR NO FERTILIZING

✔ NO STAKING

✔ MINIMAL OR NO DIVISION

✔ MINIMAL OR NO PRUNING

✔ NON-INVASIVE

DROUGHT-TOLERANT

Any garden border will benefit from the rich color, impressive size, and architectural form of *Angelica gigas*. Bonus: the flowers attract beneficial insects and bees.

Almost as striking as its red-purple flowers are the seedheads that follow; Korean angelica is biennial, blooming during the plant's second year in July and August.

The sweet pink flowers of border phlox charm alongside the strong profile of *Angelica gigas*.

## *Aralia elata* 'Aureovariegata'
# Gold-variegated aralia

**Tracy's Notes:**

**THE PLANT**
*Shrub; large yellow-edged bipinnate or tripinnate leaves; whitish flowers blooming July–August followed by black fruit*

**HARDINESS**
*Zones (3)4–9*

**HEIGHT AND SPREAD**
*10–15 ft. × 8 ft.*

**SUN AND SHADE NEEDS**
*Sun to part shade*

**COMBINES WELL WITH**
*'Island Brocade' sedge, 'Caesar's Brother' Siberian iris, and Russian sage*

*"Visitors never walk by it without asking what it is or talking about its beauty."*

Stunning, unusual, eye-catching, and spectacular could all be used to describe *Aralia elata* 'Aureovariegata'. The 8-ft. specimen that grows next to our dark brown log home glows and demands attention. Visitors never walk by it without asking what it is or talking about its beauty.

And although I admit it has a few more shortcomings than most of the other plants included in this book, it's really not overly demanding and so amazing that I feel it deserves a spot among the 50.

Gold-variegated aralia provides a bold architectural effect with its tropical-looking large (18 in. long or greater) yellow-edged bipinnate or tripinnate leaves. It is wide-spreading with a few main, course, gray stems which contain prominent leaf scars, sharp prickles, and little side branching. Give it a space where it can attain this natural habit gracefully and remain, as it is difficult to move once established.

Non-variegated root suckers appear at various locations under the canopy of the plant but these are easily pruned out while wearing gloves! Large panicles of whitish flowers appear in mid to late summer followed by black fruit which persists for a short time. Plants normally defoliate after this, which is an annoying but tolerable

Gold-variegated aralia is highlighted by plants with contrasting foliage, like this splashy canna.

Visitors to our home in Ohio rarely walk by the *Aralia elata* 'Aureovariegata' next to the house without admiring its beauty.

trait since they've been incredible for so long already. They are best not planted near a patio where debris of leaves, stems, and fruit can be a problem. Plants may be affected by spider mites. Gold-variegated aralia grows in full sun or part shade but may burn a bit in hot afternoon sun. It is difficult to find commercially and can be expensive…but aren't many things of value?

So despite having a few issues, gold-variegated aralia's high ornamental value and lack of high-maintenance traits make it a superstar for the adventurous gardener!

### Gold-variegated aralia low-maintenance checklist:

✔ LONG-LIVED

✔ TOLERATES HEAT AND HUMIDITY

✔ COLD-HARDY

✔ DEER-RESISTANT

INSECT AND DISEASE RESISTANT

✔ MINIMAL OR NO DEADHEADING

✔ MINIMAL OR NO FERTILIZING

✔ NO STAKING

✔ MINIMAL OR NO DIVISION

MINIMAL OR NO PRUNING

✔ NON-INVASIVE

✔ DROUGHT-TOLERANT

## *Aster oblongifolius var. angustatus* 'Raydon's Favorite'
# 'Raydon's Favorite' aromatic aster

I never enjoy being put on the spot to name my favorite perennial but when asked what my favorite aster is, there's no question that it's *Aster oblongifolius* var. *angustatus* 'Raydon's Favorite'. How could you not love a plant that is covered from head to toe with hundreds of cheerful small blue-violet daisylike flowers even in October, when many other plants have given up ship for the season?

How could you not love a plant that has attractive, mildew-resistant, slender, softly aromatic leaves all summer? One that is tolerant of drought and poor soil? How about one that returns dependably year after year?

I got my first 'Raydon's Favorite' in the late 1990s from Allen Bush, who introduced the plant when he owned Holbrook Farm Nursery in North Carolina. This has been my number-one aster for use in designs ever since. The huge 2- to 3-ft. by 2-ft. mounds really make a statement repeated along large borders. It's a wonderful companion to the heirloom *Dahlia* 'Thomas Edison' as they both share violet as a parent color. Plants need full sun and well-draining soil to perform their best. 'Raydon's Favorite' can be cut back by one-half in mid-June, as with other asters, and it will flower at about 2 ft. rather than 3 ft. around early to mid-October. Reseed-

**Tracy's Notes:**

**THE PLANT**
*Perennial; blue-violet daisylike flowers blooming in October; aromatic foliage*

**HARDINESS**
*Zones 4–8*

**HEIGHT AND SPREAD**
*2–3 ft. × 2 ft.*

**SUN AND SHADE NEEDS**
*Sun*

**COMBINES WELL WITH**
*'Thomas Edison' dahlia, 'September Charm' anemone, 'Cambodian Queen' chrysanthemum*

*"How could you not love a plant that has attractive, mildew-resistant, slender, softly aromatic leaves all summer?"*

ing is not normally a huge problem and division may not be needed for many years.

Try some 'Raydon's Favorite' in your garden and I think you'll have a new favorite as well.

## 'Raydon's Favorite' aromatic aster low-maintenance checklist:

✔ LONG-LIVED

✔ TOLERATES HEAT AND HUMIDITY

✔ COLD-HARDY

  DEER-RESISTANT

✔ INSECT AND DISEASE RESISTANT

✔ MINIMAL OR NO DEADHEADING

✔ MINIMAL OR NO FERTILIZING

✔ NO STAKING

✔ MINIMAL OR NO DIVISION

✔ MINIMAL OR NO PRUNING

✔ NON-INVASIVE

✔ DROUGHT-TOLERANT

'Raydon's Favorite' aromatic aster looks smashing with other late-season beauties like 'Cambodian Queen chrysanthemum.

The autumn garden can look as breathtaking as it does in spring when 'Raydon's Favorite' aromatic aster is combined with hardy chrysanthemums, tickseed, and ornamental grasses.

*Aster oblongifolius* var. *angustatus* 'Raydon's Favorite' is my number-one aster; it's a remarkably low-care perennial and its blue-violet flowers bloom all the way through October.

## *Baptisia australis*
# Blue false indigo

---

**Tracy's Notes:**

THE PLANT
*Perennial; indigo-blue flowers on spikes blooming in June; blue-green pealike leaves*

HARDINESS
*Zones 3–9*

HEIGHT AND SPREAD
*3 ft. × 4 ft.*

SUN AND SHADE NEEDS
*Sun to part shade*

COMBINES WELL WITH
*Black-eyed Susan, Siberian iris, peonies, and roses*

---

*"In the winter, blue false indigo turns black and the stems fall but I find it attractive against snow."*

---

When I started lecturing about maintenance of perennials based on the information in my first book, *The Well-Tended Perennial Garden* (Timber Press 2006), I realized that I had put *Baptisia australis* in three different areas of the talk—referencing all good things from an ease-of-maintenance point of view. First, I spoke about it as an example of a perennial that does not require frequent division. Next, I described how beautifully it responds to pruning after flowering to form a nice upright mound that doesn't need staking. Finally, I brought it up as an example of a pest-free perennial. After an amazing three mentions the light bulb went off and I got it that this tough, handsome U.S. native has it all.

*Baptisia australis* sports outstanding indigo-blue flowers in early spring on spikes that resemble a lupine, but without all the fuss and failure in growing that is experienced by most gardeners trying to grow lupines. It has waxy blue-green stems and leaves which are also three-parted. It forms a shrublike mound reaching 3 ft. high by 4 ft. wide. The blue flowers and blue-green foliage harmonize in many pastel spring color schemes especially with peonies and roses. And the summer and autumn foliage makes a great complement to many gold-flowering plants

The summer and autumn foliage of blue false indigo harmonizes well with *Rudbeckia* (black-eyed Susan) and other gold-flowering plants.

*Baptisia australis* forms a shrub-like mound reaching 3 ft. high by 4 ft. wide, and although slow to establish, is steadfast once it takes hold.

such as black-eyed Susan (*Rudbeckia*). In the winter, blue false indigo turns black and the stems fall but I find it attractive against snow.

Although slow to establish, blue false indigo is a die-hard once it takes hold. It is drought- and heat-tolerant, takes low-fertility soils, and doesn't need division for ten years or more.

Blue false indigo is often late to emerge in the spring so take care not to disturb the crowns during early spring planting. Shearing and shaping plants by one-third after flowering prevents them from flopping and opening up.

There are numerous species and cultivars of *Baptisia* now available with yellow, white, and violet-blue flowers. Once you grow it you'll be talking about it too!

## Blue false indigo low-maintenance checklist:

✔ LONG-LIVED
✔ TOLERATES HEAT AND HUMIDITY
✔ COLD-HARDY
✔ DEER-RESISTANT
✔ INSECT AND DISEASE RESISTANT
✔ MINIMAL OR NO DEADHEADING
✔ MINIMAL OR NO FERTILIZING
✔ NO STAKING
✔ MINIMAL OR NO DIVISION
✔ MINIMAL OR NO PRUNING
✔ NON-INVASIVE
✔ DROUGHT-TOLERANT

*Brunnera macrophylla* 'Jack Frost'
# 'Jack Frost' Siberian bugloss

When I asked Tony Avent, owner of Plant Delights Nursery and one of the keenest plantsmen in the country, what plants he thought would be fit for this book, he recommended *Brunnera macrophylla* 'Jack Frost'. That was the only validation I needed.

"Too cool for school," this staggeringly beautiful plant has unique silver-frosted heart-shaped leaves with contrasting green veins. The leaf surfaces create an amazing visual texture due to the intriguing pattern that is formed by the repetition of the lines of the veins. This is often described as looking like crackled porcelain. The high value of the leaves, appearing almost white at times, lights the floor of shady gardens. In the spring, baby-blue flowers like forget-me-nots dance over the sparkling foliage. After flowering the leaves continue to enlarge during the summer, eventually reaching 6 to 8 in. in diameter.

'Jack Frost' harmonizes with pastel blues and violets as well as pinks and whites. It makes dark purple foliage pop, becoming more visible under low-light conditions. Try it with some of the woodland or creeping phlox (*Phlox divaricata* and *P. stolonifera*) as well as 'Obsidian' fancy-leaf coralbells (*Heuchera* 'Obsidian'). Plants act like stars in mixed containers on shady patios.

Deer and rabbit resistance on top of minimal

**Tracy's Notes:**

**THE PLANT**
*Perennial; baby-blue flowers blooming April–May; silver-frosted heart-shaped leaves with green veins*

**HARDINESS**
*Zones 3–8*

**HEIGHT AND SPREAD**
*12–18 in. × 20 in.*

**SUN AND SHADE NEEDS**
*Part shade*

**COMBINES WELL WITH**
*Woodland or creeping phlox, 'Obsidian' fancy-leaf coralbells, and black mondo grass.*

*"The high value of the leaves, appearing almost white at times, lights the floor of shady gardens."*

care once plants are established are added bonuses. The plants grow best in high-organic soil and part shade, tolerating some morning sun in cooler regions, but prefer full shade and consistent moisture in warmer regions. Prune plants back in the spring to improve overwintering success.

'Jack Frost' was awarded Best New Perennial of the Year at the Plantarium Fair in the Netherlands and it's been chosen as a Great Plant Pick by Elizabeth Carey Miller Botanical Garden in Seattle, Washington. Tony knows his plants—yes?

## 'Jack Frost' Siberian bugloss low-maintenance checklist:

✔ LONG-LIVED

✔ TOLERATES HEAT AND HUMIDITY

✔ COLD-HARDY

✔ DEER-RESISTANT

✔ INSECT AND DISEASE RESISTANT

✔ MINIMAL OR NO DEADHEADING

✔ MINIMAL OR NO FERTILIZING

✔ NO STAKING

✔ MINIMAL OR NO DIVISION

✔ MINIMAL OR NO PRUNING

✔ NON-INVASIVE

✔ DROUGHT-TOLERANT

'Jack Frost' bugloss leaves can reach a massive 6 to 8 in. in diameter.

The black foliage of *Ophiopogon planiscapus* 'Nigrescens' is a dramatic companion to the white and green of 'Jack Frost' bugloss.

*Brunnera macrophylla* 'Jack Frost' leaves are like crackled porcelain, and harmonize well with blues, violets, pinks and whites.

## *Calamagrostis brachytricha*
# Korean feather-reed grass

**Tracy's Notes:**

**THE PLANT**
*Perennial; red-violet flowers blooming September–November; green leaves turn yellowish beige in autumn*

**HARDINESS**
*Zones 4–8*

**HEIGHT AND SPREAD**
*4 ft. × 2–3 ft.*

**SUN AND SHADE NEEDS**
*Sun to part shade*

**COMBINES WELL WITH**
*Japanese butterbur, Chinese rhubarb, and wild-oat*

> "I was thrilled when Calamagrostis brachytricha *hit the market.*"

When ornamental grasses first became popular it was fun to use them in designs and I was like a kid with a new toy. There seemed to be a shape, size, or color of grass that worked in just about any situation. However, in the early days there wasn't, to my knowledge anyway, a tall grass that could be used in the shade. I was thrilled when *Calamagrostis brachytricha* hit the market. Finally there was a tidy upright vertical form that could break the boring horizontal plane of partially shaded gardens.

And Korean feather-reed grass is not just a vertical form but also a striking accent with its clump-forming foliage and fluffy flowers on 4-ft. stems appearing in late summer. The flowers appear later and are fuller and softer than other feather reed varieties. They are tinged a lovely red-violet when they emerge, maturing to a wheat color in the autumn. The airy panicles are best positioned where they can be back or side lit. Tolerant of a wide range of soils including heavy clay in part shade or full sun, the plants benefit from afternoon shade in hot climates.

Since Korean feather-reed grass is native to moist deciduous woodlands and woodland edges, I recently combined a group of five plants with Japanese butterbur (*Petasites japonica*) and

Korean feather-reed grass loves shade, has a lovely upright form, and provides stately height.

Chinese rhubarb (*Rheum palmatum* 'Atrosanguineum') in a wet area of my garden that receives morning sun.

If you have been searching for a gorgeous grass for your shady site, then Korean feather-reed grass is definitely for you!

## Korean feather-reed grass low-maintenance checklist:

✔ LONG-LIVED

✔ TOLERATES HEAT AND HUMIDITY

✔ COLD-HARDY

✔ DEER-RESISTANT

✔ INSECT AND DISEASE RESISTANT

✔ MINIMAL OR NO DEADHEADING

✔ MINIMAL OR NO FERTILIZING

✔ NO STAKING

✔ MINIMAL OR NO DIVISION

✔ MINIMAL OR NO PRUNING

✔ NON-INVASIVE

✔ DROUGHT-TOLERANT

# *Callicarpa dichotoma*
# Purple beautyberry

Abundant clusters of striking violet fruit set this shrub apart from most other plants. It's truly a sight and one that draws great admiration. Combine this with graceful arching branches and minimal care and *Callicarpa dichotoma* is a perfect fit for the busy gardener seeking a cool, different plant.

The main care it needs is one good cut-back in the early spring since it flowers on new wood and consequently fruits on new wood. This is the hardiest species of *Callicarpa*, but its stems may die back anyway from cold winters in zone 5 if not planted in protected areas. You can coppice or stool plants by pruning them hard to 6 in. above the ground. I prune plants down to viable buds, normally about 12 in. above the base, just before they fully break to give me a bit larger framework. The plant will reach 3 to 4 ft. high in one season with the same or greater spread.

It's a fantastic addition to the autumn garden especially with asters, or try it with *Salvia leucantha* and Russian sage (*Perovskia atriplicifolia*) for a monochromatic purple color scheme. I like using the cultivar *Callicarpa dichotoma* 'Issai' as it fruits as a young plant. Cross-pollination is often needed for best fruiting so planting in a group or mass is beneficial.

**Tracy's Notes:**

**THE PLANT**
*Shrub; small pink flowers blooming June–August followed by lilac-violet fruits*

**HARDINESS**
*Zones 5–8*

**HEIGHT AND SPREAD**
*3–4 ft. × 4 ft.*

**SUN AND SHADE NEEDS**
*Sun*

**COMBINES WELL WITH**
*Mexican bush sage, Russian sage, and 'Jersey Beauty' dahlia*

*"A perfect fit for the busy gardener seeking a cool, different plant."*

Purple beautyberry has inconspicuous pink flowers in the leaf axils along the stems in the summer. Autumn color is a fair yellow. I've found that plants don't tolerate drought well. No serious pests or diseases affect the plants, although I've seen reports that they may experience leaf spot or stem diseases.

Go for the cool. Go for purple beautyberry!

## Purple beautyberry low-maintenance checklist:

✔ LONG-LIVED

✔ TOLERATES HEAT AND HUMIDITY

✔ COLD-HARDY

✔ DEER-RESISTANT

✔ INSECT AND DISEASE RESISTANT

✔ MINIMAL OR NO DEADHEADING

✔ MINIMAL OR NO FERTILIZING

✔ NO STAKING

✔ MINIMAL OR NO DIVISION

✔ MINIMAL OR NO PRUNING

✔ NON-INVASIVE

DROUGHT-TOLERANT

*Callicarpa dichotoma* 'Issai' fruits even as a young plant.

Purple beautyberry grows quickly, and can reach 3 to 4 ft. in one season.

Purple beautyberry is hard to miss with its striking violet fruit.

## Carex elata 'Aurea'
# Bowles' golden sedge

**Tracy's Notes:**

**THE PLANT**
*Perennial; yellow leaves with dark green margin*

**HARDINESS**
*Zones 5–9*

**HEIGHT AND SPREAD**
*15–18 in. × 24 in.*

**SUN AND SHADE NEEDS**
*Part to full shade*

**COMBINES WELL WITH**
*'Howell's Dwarf Tigertail' spruce, 'Blue Paradise' phlox, and European ginger*

*"It literally pulls you to it with its glowing yellow foliage."*

In the last few years I've decided I love all things carex! Like most seasoned gardeners, I go through various plant fetishes…I've had my lily, geranium, dianthus, and continuing poppy fetish but I don't see myself getting over the carex. How could I when they offer such ornamental value with such little energy expenditure?

The women who work with me in my gardens and I are always oohing and aahing over one or another carex when we are together. I think the one that impresses us the most is *Carex elata* 'Aurea'. It literally pulls you to it with its glowing yellow foliage. I have always designed it into partially shady spots where the light from the leaves is particularly phenomenal against dark soil, but it also grows in full sun. It appreciates moisture and will tolerate being slightly submerged. Plants will scorch in dry conditions or hot climates. It has 24-in. leaves that grow to about 15 to 18 in. and then arch gracefully over to the ground.

My next favorite carex would be *Carex morrowii* 'Ice Dance'. This one has creamy white leaf margins, reaches about 12 to 18 in. high, and spreads moderately by rhizomes to form a thick ground cover. Glossy evergreen leaves grace the winter garden. This is an adaptable and beautiful

The glowing yellow foliage of Bowles' golden sedge harmonizes brilliantly with perennials and woody shrubs alike.

*Carex elata* 'Aurea' (left) and fellow-shade-lover *C. morrowii* 'Ice Dance' (right) create an elegant arch over this stone edging in my garden.

plant suitable to many landscape uses in part sun to shade. Let's move on from the usual pachysandra and vinca and design in some 'Ice Dance' carex.

A few other wonderful sedges which will have you oohing and aahing include *Carex conica* 'Snowline', *C. caryophylla* 'Beatlemania', *C. dolichostachya* 'Kaga-nishiki', *C. morrowii* 'Silver Sceptre', *C. muskingumensis* 'Little Midge' and 'Oehme', *C. siderosticha* 'Shima Nishiki' (sold as island brocade), and 'Variegata'—okay, I'll stop!

## Bowles' golden sedge low-maintenance checklist:

- ✔ LONG-LIVED
- ✔ TOLERATES HEAT AND HUMIDITY
- ✔ COLD-HARDY
- ✔ DEER-RESISTANT
- ✔ INSECT AND DISEASE RESISTANT
- ✔ MINIMAL OR NO DEADHEADING
- ✔ MINIMAL OR NO FERTILIZING
- ✔ NO STAKING
- ✔ MINIMAL OR NO DIVISION
- ✔ MINIMAL OR NO PRUNING
- ✔ NON-INVASIVE
-   DROUGHT-TOLERANT

# *Ceratostigma plumbaginoides*
# Hardy plumbago

Blue is such an elusive color in garden plants. But *Ceratostigma plumbaginoides* not only offers us wonderful blue flowers in late summer and early autumn but also provides rich scarlet autumn foliage. All this wrapped up in a low-growing 8- to 12-in. spreading groundcover. What a treat!

Plants perform best with morning sun and afternoon shade. They tolerate short periods of drought and resent poorly drained soils. The only pruning that this plant requires is cutting dead stems to the ground once new growth is visible in the spring. Plants are late to emerge (sometimes not until early June at my home in central Ohio), so leave the bare stems and seedheads over the winter to mark the spot in the garden, and avoid disturbance.

Rhizomes are vigorous once established and will spread making a great groundcover with woody plants, particularly golden-foliaged ones like 'Golden Mop' Japanese falsecypress (*Chamaecyparis pisifera* 'Golden Mop'), 'Skylands' oriental spruce (*Picea orientalis* 'Skylands'), or golden bluebeard (*Caryopteris ×clandonenensis* 'Worcester Gold'). I've also seen hardy plumbago cleverly used to cover a short bank, planted with little-leaf linden trees (*Tilia cordata*) that bordered a parking lot. It looked like a blue waterfall.

**Tracy's Notes:**

**THE PLANT**
*Perennial; small blue flowers blooming July–September; green leaves turn red in autumn*

**HARDINESS**
*Zones 5–9*

**HEIGHT AND SPREAD**
*8–12 in. × 12–18 in.*

**SUN AND SHADE NEEDS**
*Sun to part shade*

**COMBINES WELL WITH**
*'Golden Mop' Japanese falsecypress, 'Skylands' oriental spruce, golden bluebeard, and little-leaf linden trees*

*"...Not only offers us wonderful blue flowers in late summer and early autumn but also provides rich scarlet autumn foliage."*

Hardy plumbago may be a bit too vigorous at times for certain other low-growing perennials such as *Coreopsis verticillata* Crème Brûlée ('Crembru'), overtaking it after a few seasons. However, it's no match for trees with shallow surface roots.

Often considered a zone 6 plant, hardy plumbago has survived well for me in zone 5 for many years now even without mulching. No pests or disease problems make adding this bit of blue to the garden even better.

### Hardy plumbago low-maintenance checklist:

✔ LONG-LIVED

✔ TOLERATES HEAT AND HUMIDITY

✔ COLD-HARDY

✔ DEER-RESISTANT

✔ INSECT AND DISEASE RESISTANT

✔ MINIMAL OR NO DEADHEADING

✔ MINIMAL OR NO FERTILIZING

✔ NO STAKING

✔ MINIMAL OR NO DIVISION

✔ MINIMAL OR NO PRUNING

✔ NON-INVASIVE

✔ DROUGHT-TOLERANT

*Ceratostigma plumbaginoides* brightens up the front of any mixed combination.

The tiny bright blue flowers of hardy plumbago bloom in late summer through early autumn.

## *Chasmanthium latifolium*
# Wild-oat

**Tracy's Notes:**

**THE PLANT**
*Perennial; olive-green foliage with oatlike flat seedheads*

**HARDINESS**
*Zones 3–8*

**HEIGHT AND SPREAD**
*2–5 ft. × 1–2 ½ ft.*

**SUN AND SHADE NEEDS**
*Sun to part shade*

**COMBINES WELL WITH**
*Large-leaved hostas, bigleaf ligularia, and 'Ogon' dawn redwood*

*"Incredible when back or side lit but even when unlit!"*

After countless attempts and failures to grow exotic and, might I add, very expensive plants in my dry and wet shade gardens, I've embraced the fortitude and spunk of *Chasmanthium latifolium*. This plant has happily made itself at home, spreading and filling in, creating a beautiful mass of foliage and seedheads in what used to be a shade area comprised mostly of holes. Sound familiar? Some people call it aggressive, due to the fact that it reseeds, but I think that's a harsh term for a plant which is better coined "assertive"!

Wild-oat is a fine-textured, mid-sized grass with olive-green bamboolike foliage that has oatlike flat seedheads which start out green then turn to bronze and finally brown. The seedheads hang on arching threadlike stems and are so delicate that they dance in the slightest breeze creating a lovely rhythm in the garden. Incredible when back or side lit but even when unlit! Seedheads remain attractive all winter and are long-lasting dried subjects.

This southern U.S. native of moist woods and stream and river edges offers an interesting textural companionship to just about any shade plant but is particularly effective with large-leaved hostas or bigleaf ligularia (*Ligularia dentata* 'Desdemona'). Plants will also grow beautifully in full sun.

Wild-oat provides a gorgeous mass of foliage and seedheads in sun or shade.

The fine-textured, olive-green bamboo-like foliage of wild-oat is beautiful in full sun.

The only thing you need to do with this plant besides enjoy it is cut it back in the early spring before new growth begins. If seedlings pop up in unwanted locations simply scratch them out at the same time.

Bring on the assertive, beautiful, easy-going plants in the garden. Bring on wild-oat!

## Wild-oat low-maintenance checklist:

✔ LONG-LIVED

✔ TOLERATES HEAT AND HUMIDITY

✔ COLD-HARDY

✔ DEER-RESISTANT

✔ INSECT AND DISEASE RESISTANT

✔ MINIMAL OR NO DEADHEADING

✔ MINIMAL OR NO FERTILIZING

✔ NO STAKING

✔ MINIMAL OR NO DIVISION

✔ MINIMAL OR NO PRUNING

✔ NON-INVASIVE

DROUGHT-TOLERANT

## *Dicentra spectabilis* 'Gold Heart'
# 'Gold Heart' bleeding heart

I had never used much of the old-fashioned bleeding heart (*Dicentra spectabilis*) in my design work in the past. For many years I had opted to use the supposedly new-and-improved fringed bleeding heart (*Dicentra formosa* 'Luxuriant'), enjoying its more refined blue-green foliage. However, I found this plant to be short-lived in most central Ohio gardens. Then along came this wonderful golden-leaved form of the old-fashioned bleeding heart and it was love at first sight. It's not only a ray of sunshine in shaded gardens, it's dependable, returning year after year!

*Dicentra spectabilis* 'Gold Heart' has golden, elegant, feathery foliage on 2-ft. mounds. Pale pink heart-shaped flowers are borne on arching spikes above the foliage. Actually I'm not crazy about the color combination of the two but its flowers have always been rather sparse so it's not a horrible thing. 'Gold Heart' is a wonderful color complement to blue hosta or the blue flowers of alpine columbine (*Aquilegia alpina*). For a twist I've interplanted 'Purple Sensation' allium (*Allium aflatunense* 'Purple Sensation') with it for shock appeal.

Early spring frost can damage the foliage so 'Gold Heart' is best planted somewhat protected among larger plants. Even if it gets hit it will

**Tracy's Notes:**

**THE PLANT**
*Perennial; golden feathery foliage; pale pink heart-shaped flowers on arching spikes blooming April–May*

**HARDINESS**
*Zones 4–9*

**HEIGHT AND SPREAD**
*2 ft. × 1 ½ ft.*

**SUN AND SHADE NEEDS**
*Part to full shade*

**COMBINES WELL WITH**
*Alpine columbine, 'Purple Sensation' allium, and black mondo grass*

*"It's not only a ray of sunshine in shaded gardens, it's dependable, returning year after year!"*

bounce back, however. Plants thrive in part to full shade and prefer moist soil although they are fairly adaptable. Avoid wet overwintering conditions. Plants will go dormant by mid to late summer but will hang around longer if soil is kept moist. All parts of the plant are slightly toxic if eaten and some gardeners have reported allergic reaction to the foliage.

This is a luminous addition to the shade or woodland garden that will steal your heart.

### 'Gold Heart' bleeding heart low-maintenance checklist:

✔ LONG-LIVED

✔ TOLERATES HEAT AND HUMIDITY

✔ COLD-HARDY

✔ DEER-RESISTANT

✔ INSECT AND DISEASE RESISTANT

✔ MINIMAL OR NO DEADHEADING

✔ MINIMAL OR NO FERTILIZING

✔ NO STAKING

✔ MINIMAL OR NO DIVISION

✔ MINIMAL OR NO PRUNING

✔ NON-INVASIVE

DROUGHT-TOLERANT

*Dicentra spectabilis* 'Gold Heart' has radiant foliage that lightens up even the shadiest of gardens.

The pale pink heart-shaped flowers of 'Gold Heart' bleeding heart bloom on arching spikes in April and May.

*Dicentra spectabilis* 'Gold Heart' bleeding heart with *Allium aflatunense* 'Purple Sensation'.

## *Dryopteris erythrosora* 'Brilliance'
# 'Brilliance' autumn fern

**Tracy's Notes:**

**THE PLANT**
*Perennial; shiny red-orange fronds mature to glossy green*

**HARDINESS**
*Zones 5–8*

**HEIGHT AND SPREAD**
*1 ½ ft. × 1 ½ ft.*

**SUN AND SHADE NEEDS**
*Part to full shade*

**COMBINES WELL WITH**
*Oakleaf hydrandgea, 'Britt-Marie Crawford' ligularia, and shredded umbrella plant*

*"Striking as a specimen on its own, yet masses of it used as a groundcover create glowing displays."*

*Dryopteris erythrosora* 'Brilliance' has quickly become my number-one choice in ferns. It's stunning, hardy, and basically requires no care. The fronds of this classy semi-evergreen fern start out a shiny red-orange and hold the color long into the season before maturing to a glossy green. They still look fantastic as I gaze out at them in the garden this mid-January day in Ohio. What a relief to see some sign of life!

The color of the fronds is a different and useful hue not often seen in plants for shade. 'Brilliance' is striking as a specimen on its own, yet masses of it used as a groundcover create glowing displays. I've found endless ways to combine it with other plants but particularly stunning is the color echo of the polished coppery new frond with the orange tomentose stems of oakleaf hydrandgea (*Hydrangea quercifolia*). Here too is a great plant to add some zest to containers in shady nooks outdoors, or it can be used equally effectively indoors.

Plants are slow-creeping and have refined compact growth, only getting 1 to 1 ½ ft. tall with an upright open habit. Fronds are distinctly triangular and pest free. Plants prefer moist humus-rich soil but appear to be more tolerant of drier soils than most ferns. Although best in part to full shade, they will tolerate some early-

'Brillance' autumn fern is an easy fit with other shade-loving plants.

morning or late-day sun but resent hot mid-day sun. In the early spring I simply prune off any brown or dead fronds that have developed over the winter and wait in anticipation for the colorful new frond show to begin.

### 'Brilliance' autumn fern low-maintenance checklist:

✔ LONG-LIVED

✔ TOLERATES HEAT AND HUMIDITY

✔ COLD-HARDY

✔ DEER-RESISTANT

✔ INSECT AND DISEASE RESISTANT

✔ MINIMAL OR NO DEADHEADING

✔ MINIMAL OR NO FERTILIZING

✔ NO STAKING

✔ MINIMAL OR NO DIVISION

✔ MINIMAL OR NO PRUNING

✔ NON-INVASIVE

DROUGHT-TOLERANT

## *Elymus hystrix*
# Bottlebrush grass

When visitors come to our gardens one of the plants they ask about most frequently is the grass with the bottlebrush-like flowers growing happily in the dry shade under a maple tree—*Elymus hystrix*, also known as *Hystrix patula*. In fact there is a tiny seedling of bottlebrush grass growing directly on our maple tree in a crevice between two large branches. Now that's what I call a tough performer!

This native grass (first introduced to me by Holden Arboretum's Roger Gettig) offers a break from the same-old, same-old look of fountain grass (*Pennisetum*) and miscanthus. It's fine and airy, creating a veil-like appearance particularly effective when backlit by the morning or late-evening sun. Flowers are green maturing to a highly valued tan that appears almost white under certain light conditions. Thin blue-gray stems carry the inflorescences high above the basal foliage to about 4 ft. starting early in the season, normally by mid-June, and seedheads are effective until late autumn. The seedheads tend to shatter over the winter but still remain somewhat ornamental, so hold off on pruning plants down until spring.

Bottlebrush grass can reseed under favorable conditions, making this a great plant for naturalized woodland or border settings. Place it where

**Tracy's Notes:**

**THE PLANT**
*Perennial; green flowers maturing to tan; blue-gray stems; seedheads resemble hedgehog quills*

**HARDINESS**
*Zones 4–8*

**HEIGHT AND SPREAD**
*3–4 ft. × 1–1 ½ ft.*

**SUN AND SHADE NEEDS**
*Sun to part shade*

**COMBINES WELL WITH**
*American ipecac, 'Gateway' Joe Pye weed, and blue false indigo*

*"Now that's what I call a tough performer!"*

you can take advantage of this seeding in a dry (or moist) partly shaded site where very little else is happy to grow. I've paired mine close to American ipecac (*Gillenia stipulata*) whose white flowers and golden autumn color harmonize with the bottlebrush grass nicely. Plants are reportedly more robust in moist fertile conditions, while dry hot sunny sites might put this cool-season grass into dormancy. Flowers are useful fresh or in dried arrangements.

If you want your friends intrigued by a plant in your garden, try incorporating some bottlebrush grass.

The foliage of *Elymus hystrix* delivers a beautiful bottle green to a garden grouping.

### Bottlebrush grass low-maintenance checklist:

✔ LONG-LIVED

✔ TOLERATES HEAT AND HUMIDITY

✔ COLD-HARDY

✔ DEER-RESISTANT

✔ INSECT AND DISEASE RESISTANT

✔ MINIMAL OR NO DEADHEADING

✔ MINIMAL OR NO FERTILIZING

✔ NO STAKING

✔ MINIMAL OR NO DIVISION

✔ MINIMAL OR NO PRUNING

✔ NON-INVASIVE

✔ DROUGHT-TOLERANT

Bottlebrush grass is spectacular when backlit by morning or late-evening sun.

## *Eryngium yuccifolium*
# Rattlesnake master

**Tracy's Notes:**

**THE PLANT**
*Perennial; greenish white flowers on narrow unbranched stems; sword- shaped spiny-margined blue-green leaves*

**HARDINESS**
*Zones 4–8*

**HEIGHT AND SPREAD**
*4 ft. × 15–18 in.*

**SUN AND SHADE NEEDS**
*Sun*

**COMBINES WELL WITH:**
*'Look Again' phlox, 'Skyracer' tall purple moor grass, 'Raydon's favorite' aromatic aster*

*"They also provide textural contrast and a strong vertical accent in combination with non-native plants in a border."*

Looking to bring a breath of the American Southwest into your garden but can't grow agaves? Seeking the feel of a sun-baked arid retreat? Then look to this low-care eastern U.S. native with its desertlike appearance and laid-back constitution to relieve that "Southern-lust."

*Eryngium yuccifolium* has semi-evergreen, sword-shaped, spiny-margined blue-green leaves resembling a yucca. The flowers, also spiny, are greenish white and borne on relatively leafless narrow unbranched 4-ft. stems. They are attractive for a long period of time, from June through September, and then they are followed by nice-looking brown seedheads which are effective through the winter.

Plants prefer sunny dry infertile conditions and since they were common in the tallgrass prairie they make great additions to native plant gardens. They also provide textural contrast and a strong vertical accent in combination with non-native plants in a border. Although they would rather grow in sand, they are normally long-lived in clay soil.

A few stems per clump usually become lax by late summer particularly in overly fertile or moist sites. Staking them looks inappropriate so I normally just prop the falling ones behind the more upright stems, live with the leaning, and

Even the dried seedheads of *Eryngium yuccifolium* are attractive and add interest to the winter garden.

Sun-lit flowers of rattlesnake master offer a nice vertical quality.

when I can't take it any more—cut them off at the base! Gloves are in order for handling plants. Plants may re-seed in ideal conditions.

Pull out the strings of chili peppers and the margaritas and plant this adaptable, eye-catching *Eryngium* in your northern garden for a Southwest feel.

### Rattlesnake master low-maintenance checklist:

✔ LONG-LIVED

✔ TOLERATES HEAT AND HUMIDITY

✔ COLD-HARDY

✔ DEER-RESISTANT

✔ INSECT AND DISEASE RESISTANT

✔ MINIMAL OR NO DEADHEADING

✔ MINIMAL OR NO FERTILIZING

✔ NO STAKING

✔ MINIMAL OR NO DIVISION

✔ MINIMAL OR NO PRUNING

✔ NON-INVASIVE

✔ DROUGHT-TOLERANT

## *Eupatorium maculatum* 'Gateway'
# 'Gateway' Joe Pye weed

**B**ig, bold, and beautiful defines this towering
North American native which lends height
and weight to a planting without being demanding. It especially shines in a stylized meadow or
naturalistic garden, and is a useful ingredient in
large mixed gardens to add often-needed scale.
*Eupatorium maculatum* 'Gateway' is usually listed
as reaching 4 ft. tall but most plants I've seen
reach 5 to 6 ft. in height. Its rosy pink, butterfly-
attracting flower heads can reach 7 to 8 in. in
diameter creating soft cloudlike forms. Plants are
remarkable viewed from above. I've designed
'Gateway' into my back border to be enjoyed
from our second-story bedroom and bathroom
windows.

This plant prefers full sun for upright growth
and moist well-drained soil, but once established
tolerates short periods of drought. It can take
two to three years to reach maturity. Plants may
exhibit leaf scorch in late summer, particularly
when subjected to extended dry periods. Pulling
your hand up the stems removes crispy critters
and tidies the plant. It responds to pruning prior
to flowering to reduce plant height. Plants can be
pinched or cut back by 6 in. during late spring to
early summer to produce shorter specimens. A
smaller-growing cultivar of *Eupatorium maculatum*
named 'Phantom' which reaches 3 ft. may be the

**Tracy's Notes:**

**THE PLANT**
*Perennial; rose-pink flower heads blooming July–September; whorled leaves*

**HARDINESS**
*Zones 2–9*

**HEIGHT AND SPREAD**
*5–6 ft. × 3–4 ft.*

**SUN AND SHADE NEEDS**
*Sun*

**COMBINES WELL WITH**
*'Herbstonne' coneflower, 'Cosmopolitan' miscanthus, and 'Iseli Foxtail' Colorado spruce*

*"Its rosy pink, butterfly-attracting flower heads can reach 7 to 8 in. in diameter creating soft cloudlike forms."*

answer if you have a smaller garden. It's new to the market as I write this so I can't guarantee its small demeanor or performance.

No deadheading is required, and plants left intact in winter offer refuge for birds. The dried seedheads are beautiful covered in frost. By spring, the tall stems may be prostrate; they usually break off easily at the plant's base for cleanup.

Add some scale and dominance to your garden—bring on 'Gateway'!

### Gateway Joe Pye weed low-maintenance checklist:

- ✔ LONG-LIVED
- ✔ TOLERATES HEAT AND HUMIDITY
- ✔ COLD-HARDY
- ✔ DEER-RESISTANT
- ✔ INSECT AND DISEASE RESISTANT
- ✔ MINIMAL OR NO DEADHEADING
- ✔ MINIMAL OR NO FERTILIZING
- ✔ NO STAKING
- ✔ MINIMAL OR NO DIVISION
- ✔ MINIMAL OR NO PRUNING
- ✔ NON-INVASIVE
- DROUGHT-TOLERANT

The flowerheads of 'Gateway' Joe Pye weed tower to 5 to 6 ft.

Cloudlike pink masses of 'Gateway' Joe Pye play a starring role in any sunny grouping.

Looking to lure butterflies? Tempt them with *Eupatorium maculatum* 'Gateway'.

*Fagus sylvatica* 'Purpurea Tricolor'
# Tricolor beech

**Tracy's Notes:**

THE PLANT
*Tree; purple leaves with rose and pink margins in spring; bronze-green with pale pink then white margins in summer; bronze-gold in autumn*

HARDINESS
*Zones 4–7*

HEIGHT AND SPREAD
*30 ft. × 20 ft.*

SUN AND SHADE NEEDS
*Sun to part shade*

COMBINES WELL WITH
*Dwarf Rocky Mountain fir, 'Perfume Counter' bearded iris, and purple-leaved ground clematis*

*"Give this plant the right spot and you'll be rewarded."*

Winters in the garden can be long and boringly monochromatic with endless grays and browns punctuated by the occasional green. Imagine the feeling of reincarnation that occurs when the bright pink leaves of tricolor beech greet you one early spring day. It is believed that pink restores youthfulness and brings people in touch with their feelings. Once you experience *Fagus sylvatica* 'Purpurea Tricolor' you'll surely be a believer in the healing powers of pink!

I planted a tricolor beech off the corner of our raised screened-in porch so that I could, quite honestly, have it near me and enjoy it at eye level even on the coldest of spring days. We have a porch light that illuminates it and it's a treat, rather than a chore, to go out in the early morning dark to feed our cats, whose bowls occupy the steps below the beech. I often recommend that clients plant this highly ornamental tree at the corner of decks or perimeter of borders.

Tricolor beech sports purple leaves that have irregular rose and pinkish margins in the spring, fading to bronze-green with pale pink then white margins in the summer, and finally bronze-gold in the autumn. This is a rather slow-growing small tree reaching 30 ft. with a somewhat narrow 20 ft. spread.

Tricolor beech captivates with the contrast of its bright pink leaves against greenery or blue sky.

It is best positioned in moist partial shade where it is protected from hot afternoon sun, otherwise its leaves can scorch; mine does every season by mid to late summer, but I tolerate it as the plant has already served its purpose and other plants in the garden then have center stage. Trees can be subject to bagworms or borers if stressed. Give this plant the right spot and you'll be rewarded.

Think pink, think tricolor beech!

## Tricolor beech low-maintenance checklist:

✔ LONG-LIVED

✔ TOLERATES HEAT AND HUMIDITY

✔ COLD-HARDY

✔ DEER-RESISTANT

✔ INSECT AND DISEASE RESISTANT

✔ MINIMAL OR NO DEADHEADING

✔ MINIMAL OR NO FERTILIZING

✔ NO STAKING

✔ MINIMAL OR NO DIVISION

✔ MINIMAL OR NO PRUNING

✔ NON-INVASIVE

DROUGHT-TOLERANT

## *Geranium* Rozanne
# Rozanne hardy geranium

I've been blown away by this relatively new geranium, sold as *Geranium* Rozanne (and also known as 'Gerwat'). It's one of the best perennials to hit the market in years and was named Perennial Plant of the Year in 2008 by the Perennial Plant Association. It flowers strongly from May to July and then moderately or sporadically until October or November without deadheading—a gardener's dream. Plants become lush and full as they reach about 18 in. tall and spread 24 to 28 in. wide. Flowers are blue-violet with a white throat and deeper violet venation.

In 2004, to create the look of a cool river running through our back garden, I lined the center path with 85 Rozanne plants. The effect was breathtaking all season as the plants spilled onto the paths. I grow Rozanne in full sun to full shade. Plants perform best in partial sun with protection from hot afternoon sun; plants in full shade flower well but get floppy. No matter the light conditions plants seem to benefit from a minor shearing after the first flush of flowers to help control legginess, promote rebloom, and create a better shape. Often side stems need to be removed to prevent crowding of other plants growing with it. Rozanne hardy geranium grows in moist soils and tolerates short periods of drought. Leave plants for the winter. In the

**Tracy's Notes:**

**THE PLANT**
Perennial; violet-blue flowers blooming May–October with purple-violet veins and small white centers

**HARDINESS**
Zones 5–8

**HEIGHT AND SPREAD**
18 in. × 24–28 in.

**SUN AND SHADE NEEDS**
Sun to part shade

**COMBINES WELL WITH**
'Summer Sun' heliopsis, 'Cambodian Queen' chrysanthemum, and 'Dragon Tails' pinellia

*"It's one of the best perennials to hit the market in years"*

spring, most stems will have broken off at the base and can be removed by hand or with light pruning.

The only disappointment I've had with Rozanne is that I've lost plants over several different winters which may be attributed to wet overwintering conditions in my clay soils. Still to me, I find it's worth it to replant this low-care geranium for the blue season-long interest it provides.

### Rozanne hardy geranium low-maintenance checklist:

LONG-LIVED

✔ TOLERATES HEAT AND HUMIDITY

✔ COLD-HARDY

DEER-RESISTANT

✔ INSECT AND DISEASE RESISTANT

✔ MINIMAL OR NO DEADHEADING

✔ MINIMAL OR NO FERTILIZING

✔ NO STAKING

✔ MINIMAL OR NO DIVISION

✔ MINIMAL OR NO PRUNING

✔ NON-INVASIVE

✔ DROUGHT-TOLERANT

Rozanne geranium can create a long-lasting river of blue-violet in any perennial border.

A close-up inspection of Rozanne geranium reveals its white throat and deeper violet venation!

*Geranium* Rozanne will wow from May through as late as November with its blue-violet showstopping flowers.

*Hakonechloa macra 'Aureola'*

# Golden-variegated Hakone grass

**Tracy's Notes:**

**THE PLANT**
Perennial; foliage striped bright yellow and green tinged with pink in autumn

**HARDINESS**
Zones 5–9

**HEIGHT AND SPREAD**
12–15 in. × 24 in.

**SUN AND SHADE NEEDS**
Partial to full shade

**COMBINES WELL WITH**
Blue hosta, purple ligularia, golden creeping Jenny

*"Give this variegated beauty moisture and shade in warm climates for best performance and you'll be delighted with its ease of care."*

This graceful grass, *Hakonechloa macra* 'Aureola', can be used to simulate the energy of the sun in shady gardens or along woodland paths. The bright yellow and green variegated leaves on compact 12- to 15-in. plants combine artistically with just about everything from blue hosta to purple ligularia. Also fine looking is golden creeping Jenny (*Lysimachia nummularia* 'Aurea') used as an underplanting to golden-variegated Hakone grass. Give this variegated beauty moisture and shade in warm climates for best performance and you'll be delighted with its ease of care.

Variegation can be affected by placement and weather, with deep shade producing more chartreuse foliage, while sun in cool climates may turn the color more creamy white than yellow (plants will only tolerate full sun in cool, moist regions). The foliage has touches of red and pink in spring and autumn weather. Clumps increase slowly by underground stems. This grass is often listed as hardy to zone 6, but it overwinters reliably in zone 5.

A cultivar of Hakone grass that I just started to use is *Hakonechloa macra* 'All Gold', and actually I've been as pleased with its color and performance as with *H. macra* 'Aureola'. Leaves are entirely yellow and it's faster-growing, more

Another cultivar of Hakone grass is *Hakonechloa macra* 'All Gold' which here makes a stunning appearance in three large pots.

'All Gold' Hakone grass is gorgeous even in winter, surrounded by snow.

robust, and slightly taller. It's gorgeous even in winter.

According to the grass guru Rick Darke in his invaluable book *The Encyclopedia of Grasses for Livable Landscapes* (Timber Press 2007), Hakone grass was historically a popular potted plant in Japan. I didn't know this at the time I used *Hakonechloa macra* 'All Gold' in three large pots for a drop-dead-gorgeous display. Also according to Rick, the green-leaved form or straight species, *H. macra*, is more sun and drought-tolerant, cold-hardy, and faster-growing than the golden forms. This is definitely something to consider for future low-care designs.

## Golden-varigated Hakone grass low-maintenance checklist:

✔ LONG-LIVED

✔ TOLERATES HEAT AND HUMIDITY

✔ COLD-HARDY

✔ DEER-RESISTANT

✔ INSECT AND DISEASE RESISTANT

✔ MINIMAL OR NO DEADHEADING

✔ MINIMAL OR NO FERTILIZING

✔ NO STAKING

✔ MINIMAL OR NO DIVISION

✔ MINIMAL OR NO PRUNING

✔ NON-INVASIVE

DROUGHT-TOLERANT

# *Helleborus*
# Hellebore

Hellebores gives gardeners chic, very early, long-lasting bloom, attractive foliage, versatility, and adaptability. The plants produce uniquely shaped and colored flowers in a delicious rainbow of hues including white, green, rose, apricot, and purple. Individual flowers can change color as they age and the sepals are attractive for a prolonged period, even after their color has faded. Foliage is normally evergreen to semi-evergreen in a fascinating assortment of glossy palmately divided or three-parted leaves. There are many hybrids and species so be sure to check out the outstanding book *Hellebores: A Comprehensive Guide* by C. Colston Burrell and Judith Knott Tyler (Timber Press 2006) for mouth-watering information and images of all things hellebore.

Hellebores are hardy, durable, and shade-tolerant. They prefer high-organic, moist well-draining, neutral-to-alkaline soils in part or dappled shade. However, they will tolerate some dry conditions in the summer, full sun if the soil is moist, and deeper shade, although flowering may be reduced.

They make handsome companions to just about any shade-loving plant including Virginia bluebells (*Mertensia virginica*), 'Gold Heart' bleeding heart (*Dicentra spectabilis* 'Gold Heart'),

**Tracy's Notes:**

**THE PLANT**
*Perennial; white, green, rose, apricot, and purple flowers blooming March–April; deep green palmate leaves*

**HARDINESS**
*Zones 4–9*

**HEIGHT AND SPREAD**
*16–18 in. × 18 in.*

**SUN AND SHADE NEEDS**
*Partial to full shade*

**COMBINES WELL WITH**
*Virginia bluebells, 'Gold Heart' bleeding heart, and barrenwort*

*"Float hellebore flowers in a shallow dish of water for a party-stopping centerpiece."*

and barrenwort (*Epimedium species*). Entertaining? Float hellebore flowers in a shallow dish of water for a party-stopping centerpiece.

Although the plants are usually evergreen, foliage can get battered by late winter. Prune off dead leaves at this time to make room for new growth and flowering. Hellebores can be prone to disease in warm, wet, humid conditions. Division is seldom if ever needed. Forms of *Helleborus* ×*hybridus* (Lenten rose) are readily available in garden centers, particularly the lovely selections 'Royal Heritage' and 'Pine Knot Select'.

Looking for the nearly ideal, ornamental, hardy shade perennial? Look no further than *Helleborus*.

Hellebore flowers are showy and spectacular—witness the rich burgundy of this *Helleborus* ×*hybridus*.

## Hellebore
## low-maintenance checklist:

✔ LONG-LIVED

✔ TOLERATES HEAT AND HUMIDITY

✔ COLD-HARDY

✔ DEER-RESISTANT

✔ INSECT AND DISEASE RESISTANT

✔ MINIMAL OR NO DEADHEADING

✔ MINIMAL OR NO FERTILIZING

✔ NO STAKING

✔ MINIMAL OR NO DIVISION

✔ MINIMAL OR NO PRUNING

✔ NON-INVASIVE

✔ DROUGHT-TOLERANT

The rainbow array of colors and attractive evergreen foliage of hellebores are a must-have for any garden.

# *Hosta* 'Sum and Substance'
# 'Sum and Substance' hosta

**Tracy's Notes:**

**THE PLANT**
*Perennial; large chartreuse to gold leaves; spikes of pale lavender flowers bloom in August*

**HARDINESS**
*Zones 3–8*

**HEIGHT AND SPREAD**
*2 ½ ft. × 4–5 ft.*

**SUN AND SHADE NEEDS**
*Partial to full shade*

**COMBINES WELL WITH:**
*Rozanne hardy geranium, purple snakeroot, and 'Molly Sanderson' violet*

*"The award-winning hosta that's still the golden grandmamma of them all is the big, the bodacious,* Hosta *'Sum and Substance'."*

In the hosta world today there are a "kajillion" varieties available to gardeners and new ones appear at such a rapid rate that it's challenging for even the most devout hostaphile to stay in the loop. But through all the excitement over this new one or that new one, the award-winning hosta that's still the golden grandmamma of them all is the big, the bodacious, *Hosta* 'Sum and Substance'.

This goliath can form an immense clump to 2 ½ ft. or more high by 4 to 5 ft. wide (reports have been made of a 9-ft. spread—but excited gardeners can sometimes exaggerate!). Leaves are yellow or chartreuse, corrugated, and heart-shaped, measuring 12 to 15 in. or greater in width by 20 in. or so in length. Attractive pale lavender flowers are borne on 50-in. somewhat droopy stems above the foliage in late summer.

This beauty, best suited as a specimen, adds weight and dominance to gardens so often needed to anchor plantings that are usually filled with numerous fine, soft-textured plants. Filtered shade, such as is provided by high overhead trees, is ideal for best coloring, but it also tolerates heavier shade. 'Sum and Substance' enjoys morning sun and actually is more tolerant of sun than most hostas but can still scorch in hot afternoon sun. It's also yummy planted in bright-

With its dinner-plate-sized leaves, 'Sum and Substance' hosta is extraordinary when grouped with contrasting foliage of other plants, like *Cimcifuga racemosa*.

ly colored large ceramic pots.

Slugs and hostas normally go hand-in-hand but *Hosta* 'Sum and Substance' has such thick, heavy leaves that they are normally resistant to slugs and snails, making them a great addition to the easy-care list. If you prefer big blue over big yellow and want a slug-resistant hosta, go for *Hosta* 'Big Daddy', *H.* 'Blue Angel', or *H.* 'Love Pat'.

Confused over the flood of new hostas? Look no further than the tried-and-true *Hosta* 'Sum and Substance'!

### 'Sum and Substance' hosta low-maintenance checklist:

- ✔ LONG-LIVED
- ✔ TOLERATES HEAT AND HUMIDITY
- ✔ COLD-HARDY
-   DEER-RESISTANT
- ✔ INSECT AND DISEASE RESISTANT
- ✔ MINIMAL OR NO DEADHEADING
- ✔ MINIMAL OR NO FERTILIZING
- ✔ NO STAKING
- ✔ MINIMAL OR NO DIVISION
- ✔ MINIMAL OR NO PRUNING
- ✔ NON-INVASIVE
-   DROUGHT-TOLERANT

*Hydrangea macrophylla* Endless Summer
# Endless Summer hydrangea

This charming hydrangea, sold as Endless Summer and also known as 'Bailmer', has giant mophead blooms in pink, blue, or sometimes a lovely blending of the two, flowers for seven months or more in northern and southern gardens, and is a dream for gardeners, plant marketers, and watercolorists! Massive 8- to 10-in. flower heads will have you ecstatic and supporting the notion that "bigger is better." Daily I have to walk over to my planting of these darlings to see how the buds are opening or how the seedheads are maturing and progressing through a kaleidoscope of tints, tones, and shades. Properly grown they just reek with positive energy and have me tempted to be a shrub-hugger!

Endless Summer hydrangea has the ability to bloom on new as well as old wood, so if there is winter dieback or frost-kill in the early spring, plants will still bloom on new wood that is produced. This plant is ideal for foundations (particularly sweet against white houses), containers, or the mixed border, reaching a rounded 3 to 5 ft., and combines beautifully with pastel or cool-colored plants such as Rozanne hardy geranium (*Geranium* Rozanne, or 'Gerwat'), 'Homestead Purple' verbena (*Verbena canadensis* 'Homestead Purple'), or 'Pink Beauty' boltonia

## Tracy's Notes:

**THE PLANT**
*Shrub; large clusters of blue or pink summer flowers blooming July–September; dark green serrated leaves*

**HARDINESS**
*Zones 4–9*

**HEIGHT AND SPREAD**
*3–5 ft × 3–4 ft.*

**SUN AND SHADE NEEDS**
*Sun to part shade*

**COMBINES WELL WITH**
*Rozanne hardy geranium, 'Homestead Purple' verbena, and 'Pink Beauty' boltonia*

*"Properly grown they just reek with positive energy and have me tempted to be a shrub-hugger!"*

(*Boltonia asteroides* 'Pink Beauty').

Endless Summer prefers dappled shade or morning sun with shelter from hot afternoon sun. I have mine in a large border where it gets morning light and then is sheltered from harsh afternoon light by a large clump of *Miscanthus sinensis* 'Malepartus'. Flowers can be used fresh or dry.

Blooms will be pink in alkaline soil and blue in acidic. In my neutral soil I add a couple of cups of aluminum sulfate in the early spring and I'm rewarded with a striking combination of flower colors. There are products on the market that can help produce blue or pink flowers. In the midwestern United States, plants are often hit by winter cold. Prune damaged branches down to viable buds in the spring after danger of frost has passed.

### Endless Summer hydrangea low-maintenance checklist:

✔ LONG-LIVED

✔ TOLERATES HEAT AND HUMIDITY

✔ COLD-HARDY

DEER-RESISTANT

✔ INSECT AND DISEASE RESISTANT

✔ MINIMAL OR NO DEADHEADING

✔ MINIMAL OR NO FERTILIZING

✔ NO STAKING

✔ MINIMAL OR NO DIVISION

✔ MINIMAL OR NO PRUNING

✔ NON-INVASIVE

DROUGHT-TOLERANT

Bigger is better! Endless Summer hydrangea delivers with its giant mophead blooms in pink, blue, and sometimes even a blend of the two.

Depending on soil pH, Endless Summer hydrangea can bloom in full pink.

Few plants compare with the charm and beauty of Endless Summer hydrangea.

## *Indocalamus tessellatus*
# Bigleaf bamboo

**Tracy's Notes:**

**THE PLANT**
*Perennial; giant leaves up to 4"
wide and 24" long*

**HARDINESS**
*Zones (5)6–9*

**HEIGHT AND SPREAD**
*3–7 ft. × 2 ½–6 ft.*

**SUN AND SHADE NEEDS**
*Sun to part shade*

**COMBINES WELL WITH**
*Gold-variegated aralia,
Persian ironwood, and fernleaf
fullmoon maple*

*"It's gorgeous in pots
on a shaded patio,
screened-in porch, near
water features, or as an
indoor plant."*

All of us who work with computers are familiar with the phrase "user error." We could apply this to gardeners (the user) and plants (the device) as well. My case in point here is *Indocalamus tessellatus*.

Bigleaf bamboo has a tropical quality, providing extraordinary form and texture. Plants that have been in my Midwest garden since 2000 are 30 to 36 in. tall and have leaves that are 15 in. long by 2 to 3 in. wide. The leaves can reach a length of 2 ft. and a width of 4 in., and plants can attain 7 ft. in warmer climates.

It is a slightly slower-spreading, less-aggressive bamboo than many other "running" bamboo. My clump slowly increased at first then picked up speed in the fifth season. It now covers about a 5- to 6-ft. area. In lighter sandy soils spread may be faster. Now comes the proper way to use it—design this cool plant into spaces where you can take advantage of this spreading habit as a luxurious ground cover on a shady bank, or as an unexpected candidate (dump the impatiens!) for the narrow beds next to buildings surrounded completely by sidewalks or hardscaping to contain its spread. It's gorgeous in pots on a shaded patio, screened-in porch, near water features, or as an indoor plant.

If you do use it in a mixed border, the main

Bigleaf bamboo brings some green to a snowy winter season.

When the autumn colors are at their best, bigleaf bamboo provides a vibrant green contrast.

maintenance will be to annually remove runners as they encroach on other plants. A barrier could be placed at the time of planting to contain clumps.

Plants are semi-evergreen to evergreen and don't look tatty until about late April to mid-May. Just prune off the bad leaves at this time; never cut plants down to the ground.

### Bigleaf bamboo low-maintenance checklist:

✔ LONG-LIVED

✔ TOLERATES HEAT AND HUMIDITY

   COLD-HARDY

✔ DEER-RESISTANT

✔ INSECT AND DISEASE RESISTANT

✔ MINIMAL OR NO DEADHEADING

✔ MINIMAL OR NO FERTILIZING

✔ NO STAKING

✔ MINIMAL OR NO DIVISION

✔ MINIMAL OR NO PRUNING

✔ NON-INVASIVE

✔ DROUGHT-TOLERANT

## *Iris sibirica* 'Caesar's Brother'
# 'Caesar's Brother' Siberian iris

When people think of iris, visions of the tall bearded forms which perhaps grew in their grandmother's garden may often come to mind. But when I think of iris I look to the more delicately flowered, trouble-free, adaptable Siberian iris and in particular the rich deep violet flowering *Iris sibirica* 'Caesar's Brother'. This old award-winning cultivar is still a crowd pleaser and my favorite because few others can compete with its sumptuous color and vigor.

While the foliage of bearded iris (*Iris germanica*) declines mid-season, often riddled with pests and disease, the grasslike, vase-shaped, pest-free foliage of 'Caesar's Brother' provides strong structural lines throughout the season. In the autumn it goes one step further and takes on a beautiful golden glow. Bearded iris flowers turn to mush and require regular deadheading while 'Caesar's Brother' produces magnificent ornamental seed pods.

These fleshy rooted plants are tolerant of a variety of soil conditions including just about everything from moist, boglike sites to dry infertile areas. They will grow in partial shade but will flop if grown in too much shade. Plants don't normally require division for six to ten years after planting. In the spring the entire plant can be cut down. Deadheading at least one third

**Tracy's Notes:**

**THE PLANT**
*Perennial; deep violet flowers blooming in May; straplike leaves*

**HARDINESS**
*Zones 3–9*

**HEIGHT AND SPREAD**
*2 ½–3 ft. × 2 ft.*

**SUN AND SHADE NEEDS**
*Sun to part shade*

**COMBINES WELL WITH**
*Princess Victoria Louise poppy, 'Nice Gal' peony, and comeliancherry dogwood*

*"It's stunning en masse along a pond or as a specimen next to a small water garden."*

of the seedheads may lead to a better flowering plant the following season.

'Caesar's Brother' is spectacular in late May to early June coordinated with Princess Victoria Louise poppy (*Papaver orientale* 'Prinzessin Victoria Louise') or 'Nice Gal' peony (*Paeonia* 'Nice Gal'). It's stunning *en masse* along a pond or as a specimen next to a small water garden. It attracts butterflies and is usually deer-resistant.

The next time you think iris, look to the care-free, multiseasonal *Iris sibirica* 'Caesar's Brother', which never goes out of fashion.

**'Caesar's Brother' Siberian iris low-maintenance checklist:**

✔ LONG-LIVED

✔ TOLERATES HEAT AND HUMIDITY

✔ COLD-HARDY

✔ DEER-RESISTANT

✔ INSECT AND DISEASE RESISTANT

✔ MINIMAL OR NO DEADHEADING

✔ MINIMAL OR NO FERTILIZING

✔ NO STAKING

✔ MINIMAL OR NO DIVISION

✔ MINIMAL OR NO PRUNING

✔ NON-INVASIVE

✔ DROUGHT-TOLERANT

'Caesar's Brother' Siberian iris has it all—remarkable looks, stupendous color, and a strong vertical profile.

*Iris sibirica* 'Caesar's Brother' is a stunning form that looks great for months on end.

# *Itea virginica* 'Henry's Garnet'
# 'Henry's Garnet' Virginia sweet spire

**Tracy's Notes:**

**THE PLANT**
*Shrub; large fragrant white flowers blooming May–June and green foliage turning reddish purple in autumn*

**HARDINESS**
*Zones 5–9*

**HEIGHT AND SPREAD**
*3–5 ft. × 3–5 ft.*

**SUN AND SHADE NEEDS**
*Sun to part shade*

**COMBINES WELL WITH**
*'September Charm' Japanese anemone, serviceberry trees, and 'Lucifer' crocosmia*

*"I've used the straight species* Itea virginica *in my design work and gardens for as long as I can remember."*

Let's see…a cold- and heat-hardy, pest-free 3- to 5-ft. tall deciduous shrub with fragrant white early-summer flowers, followed by rich red-purple autumn color, that grows in sun or shade, wet or dry soils—that certainly makes *Itea virginica* 'Henry's Garnet' a no-brainer pick for just about any garden.

I've used the straight species *Itea virginica* in my design work and gardens for as long as I can remember. It was always one of the top shrubs I'd select for outlining structure in combination with shade-loving perennials. It also provided season-long interest and I could guarantee it with no question. This U.S. native has a beautiful mix of red, orange, and yellow autumn color and grows just slightly taller and wider than the selection 'Henry's Garnet'.

Now 'Henry's Garnet' has pretty much taken over the market due to the fact that it's more compact, the flowers are larger, the autumn color more intense and uniform, and it appears to be slightly hardier than straight *Itea virginica*. The 4- to 6-in.-long white, late-June flowers combine nicely with just about everything. And the autumn color is really amazing with Japanese anemone, particularly *Anemone hupehensis* 'September Charm', or when used as an underplanting to serviceberry trees (*Amelanchier* species).

Come autumn, Virginia sweet spire brings it on with a gorgeous display of red, orange, and yellow.

Plants perform well in most landscape sites and are effective placed near a porch, deck, or front entrance where the light flower fragrance can be appreciated. They are also at home in a woodland or naturalized setting, and if given a moist or wet location they can sucker to colonize a sizeable area.

Still racking your brain over what would be a great shrub? Relax and choose *Itea virginica* 'Henry's Garnet'.

### 'Henry's Garnet' Virginia sweet spire low-maintenance checklist:

✔ LONG-LIVED

✔ TOLERATES HEAT AND HUMIDITY

✔ COLD-HARDY

✔ DEER-RESISTANT

✔ INSECT AND DISEASE RESISTANT

✔ MINIMAL OR NO DEADHEADING

✔ MINIMAL OR NO FERTILIZING

✔ NO STAKING

✔ MINIMAL OR NO DIVISION

✔ MINIMAL OR NO PRUNING

✔ NON-INVASIVE

✔ DROUGHT-TOLERANT

## *Ligularia dentata* 'Britt-Marie Crawford'
# 'Britt-Marie Crawford' ligularia

Talk about a colorist's dream! I went gaga when I first saw this plant. It was a "drive-by" spotting. I was riding on a golf cart while shopping at a wholesale perennial nursery when I spied a block of containers of these plants across the nursery yard and screeched to the poor unsuspecting salesman driving the cart, "What's *that*?" My passion for *Ligularia dentata* 'Britt-Marie Crawford' hasn't waned, but instead has grown stronger as I see how durable it is and as I thrill in the creativity of artistic combinations that can be made with it.

The large, dramatic, lustrous dark chocolate-maroon rounded leaves are violet underneath and are nothing short of captivating even when performing solo. But think of the endless combinations and fun you can have with it. I'm particularly fond of a complementary color scheme involving 'Britt-Marie Crawford' with 'Golden Tutsan' St. Johnswort (*Hypericum androsaemum* 'Golden Tutsan'). Yellow-orange daisylike flowers are produced in the summer and create instant contrast. Another rich duo is between 'Britt-Marie Crawford' and the copper fronds of 'Brilliance' autumn fern (*Dryopteris erythrosora* 'Brilliance').

To help meet the plant's requirement for moisture I "bag" it. After digging the hole for the

### Tracy's Notes:

**THE PLANT**
Perennial; dark chocolate-maroon rounded leaves, violet underneath; golden yellow daisylike flowers

**HARDINESS**
Zones 4–8

**HEIGHT AND SPREAD**
3–4 ft. × 3–4 ft.

**SUN AND SHADE NEEDS**
Part shade to shade

**COMBINES WELL WITH**
'Golden Tutsan' St. Johnswort, 'Brilliance' autumn fern, and toad lily

*"Lustrous dark chocolate-maroon rounded leaves are violet underneath and are nothing short of captivating even when performing solo."*

plant, line it with a plastic garbage bag, poke a couple of holes in the bottom of the bag, and backfill with high-organic soil and plant. This procedure improves the success rate even during short dry periods. Plants will tolerate morning sun, which is a vision viewed through the leaves, but resent hot afternoon sun which can cause wilting. High dappled shade is acceptable. Young leaves may be delicacies for slugs and snails. Apply an organic bait at leaf emergence if needed.

Add an artistic touch to your garden with this theatrical drama queen. It will have you gaga too!

## 'Britt-Marie Crawford' ligularia low-maintenance checklist:

✔ LONG-LIVED

✔ TOLERATES HEAT AND HUMIDITY

✔ COLD-HARDY

✔ DEER-RESISTANT

✔ INSECT AND DISEASE RESISTANT

✔ MINIMAL OR NO DEADHEADING

✔ MINIMAL OR NO FERTILIZING

✔ NO STAKING

✔ MINIMAL OR NO DIVISION

✔ MINIMAL OR NO PRUNING

✔ NON-INVASIVE

DROUGHT-TOLERANT

The unusual dark chocolate-maroon leaves of 'Britt-Marie Crawford' draw the eye and create instant contrast with green foliage plants, like 'Brilliance' autumn fern.

*Ligularia dentata* 'Britt-Marie Crawford' adds an astonishing punch to just about any combination, or even solo.

*Lonicera periclymenum* 'Graham Thomas'

# 'Graham Thomas' woodbine honeysuckle

**Tracy's Notes:**

**THE PLANT**
*Woody vine; extremely fragrant light yellow flowers blooming June–September, with red fruit*

**HARDINESS**
*Zones 4–8*

**HEIGHT AND SPREAD**
*20 ft. × 10–15 ft.*

**SUN AND SHADE NEEDS**
*Sun to part shade*

**COMBINES WELL WITH**
*'Polish Spirit' clematis, purple beautyberry, and 'Color Guard' yucca*

*"This hummingbird magnet is unforgettable associated with purples and blues."*

It's great if a plant is beautiful and easy to grow but it's an added bonus if it can evoke memories and stir emotion. That's just what *Lonicera periclymenum* 'Graham Thomas' can do. A large vine covers the trellis on the front of our log home. Its seductive fragrance fills the air in the evenings, permeating the windows of our house and the air surrounding our front porch. It's a scent I now associate with the peace of home and family.

Soft creamy yellow tubular flowers borne in whirled clusters cover the plant in June and July, continuing sporadically throughout the summer with a few even into the autumn. Flower buds begin white and the yellow color deepens with time. A few small red berries may follow.

This hummingbird magnet is unforgettable associated with purples and blues. Try planting the purple-flowering 'Polish Spirit' clematis (*Clematis* 'Polish Spirit') at its base and let the two intertwine for a pleasing flowering wall, or fence. I attached custom painted trellis to a condominium fence for a client and have these vines along with some climbing roses growing on it. The fragrance is intense in the intimate space. Plants can be vigorous so periodic heading back is required to keep vines intact in smaller-scale settings.

Each summer our log home is filled with the seductive fragrance of 'Graham Thomas', and the hummingbirds love it, too.

Best flowering occurs in sun or partial shade. Plants are very adaptable to various soils, drought, heat, and humidity, and are also reportedly deer-resistant. Tip dieback can occur in zone 5 during severe winters. Prune off damage and plants recover nicely. After many years harder pruning may be necessary in the spring to remove some inner dead vines on large plants.

This charming old-fashioned plant named for the late renowned English plantsman Graham Thomas was awarded the Royal Horticultural Society's Award of Garden Merit.

Plant a memory, plant 'Graham Thomas'.

### 'Graham Thomas' woodbine honeysuckle low-maintenance checklist:

✔ LONG-LIVED

✔ TOLERATES HEAT AND HUMIDITY

✔ COLD-HARDY

DEER-RESISTANT

✔ INSECT AND DISEASE RESISTANT

✔ MINIMAL OR NO DEADHEADING

✔ MINIMAL OR NO FERTILIZING

✔ NO STAKING

✔ MINIMAL OR NO DIVISION

✔ MINIMAL OR NO PRUNING

✔ NON-INVASIVE

✔ DROUGHT-TOLERANT

# *Metasequoia glyptostroboides* 'Ogon'
# 'Ogon' dawn redwood

Most of us seem to love plants that have been blessed with the Midas touch. In fact, among my 50 choices I'm sure you'll notice somewhat of a pattern featuring plants with completely yellow or yellow-variegated leaves. They are captivating, after all; 'Gold Heart' bleeding heart, variegated aralia, and 'Ogon' acorus represent just a few. However this is an "ogon" (Japanese word for gold) of a different animal. While *Acorus graminius* 'Ogon' reaches a foot or less in height, *Metasequoia glyptostroboides* 'Ogon' (also known as 'Gold Rush') can possibly reach 50 ft. or more. Its golden foliage combined with its stately size creates a staggering specimen.

'Ogon' is a relatively fast-growing, pyramidal, deciduous conifer with a fairly narrow spread (15 ft.). This makes it an incredible addition to the large garden or border where it can provide scale. Its fine texture and airy nature make it appear quite light in weight relative to its size. I have one planted in the far corner of my back garden. It's right on the edge of the border and makes for a smooth transition to the wooded area beyond. There is a pleasing flow from the 'Ogon' down to the 6-ft. tall 'Gateway' Joe Pye weed and lavender mist meadow rue (*Thalictrum rochebruneanum*) growing with it. Also consider using this plant as a lawn tree, on golf courses,

**Tracy's Notes:**

**THE PLANT**
*Tree; yellow-green changing to bronze in autumn, finely textured foliage and peeling bark; prominent winter buds.*

**HARDINESS**
*Zones 4–8*

**HEIGHT AND SPREAD**
*50 ft. × 15 ft.*

**SUN AND SHADE NEEDS**
*Sun*

**COMBINES WELL WITH**
*'Gateway' Joe Pye weed, lavender mist meadow rue, and golden catalpa*

*"Its golden foliage combined with its stately size creates a staggering specimen."*

or as a distinctive addition to public spaces surrounding tall buildings.

The foliage color softens slightly to a yellow-green as the season progresses and finally to a notable bronze in the autumn. The tree's attractive shredded reddish brown bark adds an additional unique color dimension for combos with other plants. Plants are adaptable to soil but prefer moist locations and tolerate summer heat.

As you can see, 'Ogon' dawn redwood is worth its weight in gold!

## 'Ogon' dawn redwood low-maintenance checklist:

✔ LONG-LIVED

✔ TOLERATES HEAT AND HUMIDITY

✔ COLD-HARDY

   DEER-RESISTANT

✔ INSECT AND DISEASE RESISTANT

✔ MINIMAL OR NO DEADHEADING

✔ MINIMAL OR NO FERTILIZING

✔ NO STAKING

✔ MINIMAL OR NO DIVISION

✔ MINIMAL OR NO PRUNING

✔ NON-INVASIVE

   DROUGHT-TOLERANT

'Ogon' dawn redwood's golden foliage brightens up the garden and provides a nice transition from borders to wooded areas.

'Ogon' dawn redwood dazzles even during the chill of autumn with its narrow spread of bronze foliage.

*Metasequoia glyptostroboides* 'Ogon' impresses with its incredible height—up to 50 ft.—but its light, airy texture keeps it from being too imposing.

# *Miscanthus sinensis* var. *condensatus* 'Cosmopolitan'
# 'Cosmopolitan' miscanthus

**Tracy's Notes:**

**THE PLANT**
*Perennial; mid-green and white variegated leaves; blooms emerge coppery red in September then fade to tan*

**HARDINESS**
*Zones (5)6–9*

**HEIGHT AND SPREAD**
*6–10 ft. × 4–5 ft.*

**SUN AND SHADE NEEDS**
*Sun*

**COMBINES WELL WITH**
*Dwarf Rocky Mountain fir, 'Jersey Beauty' dahlia, 'Blue Paradise' phlox, 'Royal Purple' smoke tree, and Formosa lily*

*"White is light and bright, it creates a feeling of space, and comes alive in the evenings."*

Are you looking for a classy, sophisticated (dare I say cosmopolitan?) plant to match your cosmopolitan or even not-so-cosmopolitan lifestyle? Then consider adding this luminous variegated miscanthus to your garden's repertoire.

Although there are loads of beautiful easy-care grasses, *Miscanthus sinensis* var. *condensatus* 'Cosmopolitan' has always been particularly popular due to its resplendent foliage. The leaves are wider than the standard miscanthus, with mid-green centers and variegated white margins. Its crisp, clean lines are powerful but not gaudy and work nicely in cool color schemes with blues and violets as well as with soft pinks and yellows and of course other whites. I've combined it effectively with dwarf Rocky Mountain fir (*Abies lasiocarpa* var. *arizonica* 'Compacta'), 'Jersey Beauty' dahlia (*Dahlia* 'Jersey Beauty'), 'Blue Paradise' phlox (*Phlox paniculata* 'Blue Paradise'), and Formosa lily (*Lilium formosanum*).

Keep in mind that other colors deepen and increase in contrast and saturation against the white on this grass. Dark colors create a large degree of contrast with white and form prominent focal points. Consider pairing 'Cosmopolitan' miscanthus with 'Royal Purple' smoke tree (*Cotinus coggygria* 'Royal Purple') for such effect.

This award-winning plant (judged so by the Royal Horticultural Society, no less) will command attention in even the busiest of borders.

White is light and bright, it creates a feeling of space, and comes alive in the evenings. 'Cosmopolitan' miscanthus is brilliant for gardens of busy working people who may only be able to enjoy the garden late in the day. Consider it to jazz up restaurant or nightclub entrances.

This is an award-winning plant, having received an Award of Garden Merit from England's Royal Horticultural Society. Plants are upright 6 to 10 ft., non-flopping, robust growers. Copper-colored plumes develop in mid-September and rarely develop fertile seed except in truly warmer regions, removing the plant from invasive concerns associated with some other miscanthus.

Turn on the light at night in your garden with this incandescent cosmopolitan plant.

### 'Cosmopolitan' miscanthus low-maintenance checklist:

✔ LONG-LIVED

✔ TOLERATES HEAT AND HUMIDITY

✔ COLD-HARDY

✔ DEER-RESISTANT

✔ INSECT AND DISEASE RESISTANT

✔ MINIMAL OR NO DEADHEADING

✔ MINIMAL OR NO FERTILIZING

✔ NO STAKING

✔ MINIMAL OR NO DIVISION

✔ MINIMAL OR NO PRUNING

✔ NON-INVASIVE

✔ DROUGHT-TOLERANT

## *Molinia caerulea* subsp. *arundinacea* 'Skyracer'
# 'Skyracer' tall purple moor grass

This is by far my favorite ornamental grass, and I keep talking and writing about it in the hopes it will receive the attention it deserves. Delicate panicles of *Molinia caerulea* subsp. *arundinacea* 'Skyracer' soar to a height of 7 or 8 ft., yet plants remain compact, growing only about 3 ft. wide with 2- to 3-ft. high foliage. These dimensions make 'Skyracer' well-suited to situations where height and scale are needed but space won't allow a wider, heavier plant. This is usually the case in restricted border spaces located adjacent to large homes or tall apartment buildings. If planted near sidewalks expect some stems to arch over and tickle passersby.

It makes a great see-through plant so it also works beautifully along the front edge of a sunny border where it can be viewed up close. Place it where it may be backlit or sidelit to show off its panicles, or where a light breeze will create poetry in motion. Its outstanding yellow autumn foliage is an added bonus. The veil-like fine airy texture on such a tall plant is rare and it complements just about anything. It's particularly nice as a lightweight addition to a shrub border.

Stems eventually break at the base in winter, but I enjoy seeing their sprawling outlines on the

**Tracy's Notes:**

THE PLANT
*Perennial; golden tan inflorescences on tall wiry stems; green foliage turns yellow in autumn*

HARDINESS
*Zones 4–9*

HEIGHT AND SPREAD
*7–8 ft. × 3 ft.*

SUN AND SHADE NEEDS
*Sun*

COMBINES WELL WITH:
*'Alluring Peach' daylily, rattlesnake master, and dwarf conifers*

*"Place it where it may be backlit or sidelit to show off its panicles, or where a light breeze will create poetry in motion."*

ground. I cut this plant back in the spring, but it can also be sheared in late autumn or early winter which will be needed if grown in small spaces. This grass is adaptable but may be prone to foliar disease in the extreme heat and humidity of the southern United States.

'Skyracer' tall purple moor grass is living art in the garden.

## 'Skyrace' tall purple moor grass low-maintenance checklist:

✔ LONG-LIVED

✔ TOLERATES HEAT AND HUMIDITY

✔ COLD-HARDY

✔ DEER-RESISTANT

✔ INSECT AND DISEASE RESISTANT

✔ MINIMAL OR NO DEADHEADING

✔ MINIMAL OR NO FERTILIZING

✔ NO STAKING

✔ MINIMAL OR NO DIVISION

✔ MINIMAL OR NO PRUNING

✔ NON-INVASIVE

DROUGHT-TOLERANT

The airy texture of 'Skyracer' harmonizes with smaller, more compact plants and is a lightweight but substantial addition to a mixed border.

Not many plants look much better when sunlit than the long stems of 'Skyracer' combine with a light breeze create a wonderful sense of movement.

## Paeonia obovata
# Woodland peony

**Tracy's Notes:**

**THE PLANT**
*Perennial; shiny red and blue-black fruit; small pink flowers blooming in May; dark green narrow, divided leaves with good fall color*

**HARDINESS**
*Zones 4–8*

**HEIGHT AND SPREAD**
*1 ½–2 ft. × 1 ½–2 ft.*

**SUN AND SHADE NEEDS**
*Part shade to shade*

**COMBINES WELL WITH:**
*'Jack Frost' Siberian bugloss, hellebore, and varigated Solomon's seal*

*"Seductive red and blue-black fruit that will raise the heartbeat of the most sedate of gardeners."*

This is not your grandparents' peony, unless they were some rockin' plant nerds. We're not talking about the typical huge flowers on plants often seen growing in the middle of open lawns from properties of yesteryear. We are talking about a shade-loving woodland species with small, single, pink flowers. Seductive red and blue-black fruit that will raise the heartbeat of the most sedate of gardeners.

Come on, how cool is this scenario? In late summer to early autumn, when things are pretty quiet in shady places, an intense succulent red amid leaf after leaf of hosta, fern, and ivy catches the eye of the dazed plant-tender. There is a magnetic pull to the color and the gardener serpentines, in scuffed wellies, weeding knife in hand, through the jungle of foliage, to be rewarded by the sight of the tantalizing fruit which is almost unbelievable. What can it be? It's not a viburnum, is it? No, it's not a viburnum (nuts, wrong again)…it's *Paeonia obovata*, the little-known woodland peony. And this isn't something you can buy out of the J. Peterman catalog but don't despair, it's something you'll find in several rare plant catalogs—praise the Lord!

Okay, back to reality—the leaves of *Paeonia obovata* are divided into seven to nine egg-

The seductive fruit of *Paonia obovata* add a decidedly exotic touch to even the most ordinary garden combination.

shaped leaflets. Its flower buds are attractively round, opening in the spring. The species is native to Japan and China. It tolerates morning sun and light to medium shade. Foliage can get a bit tatty by late season.

Buck the trend and be the hip grandparents of future generations: plant this adventure-novel-worthy peony in your garden.

## Woodland peony low-maintenance checklist:

✔ LONG-LIVED

✔ TOLERATES HEAT AND HUMIDITY

✔ COLD-HARDY

✔ DEER-RESISTANT

✔ INSECT AND DISEASE RESISTANT

✔ MINIMAL OR NO DEADHEADING

✔ MINIMAL OR NO FERTILIZING

✔ NO STAKING

✔ MINIMAL OR NO DIVISION

✔ MINIMAL OR NO PRUNING

✔ NON-INVASIVE

✔ DROUGHT-TOLERANT

## *Panicum virgatum* 'Rehbraun'
# 'Rehbraun' switchgrass

*Panicum virgatum* 'Rehbraun' is just one of the many outstanding selections of switchgrass available for gardeners today. As a cultivar of *Panicum virgatum*, which was a component of the American tallgrass prairie, it offers not only beauty but also resilience, versatility, incredible adaptability, and ease of care.

'Rehbraun' switchgrass grows as a sturdy clump of fine-textured leaves and flower panicles. Its form provides weight in the garden but with a light, soft, airy, almost translucent outline. This is effective in blurring boundaries and creating a sense of greater space around it. It is a restful yet intricate place for the eye to pause when used as a specimen in busy mixed gardens. The panicles create an ethereal mistlike appearance when viewed from a distance, particularly when covered in morning dew or backlit by the sun. This effect is breathtaking when plants are used *en masse* in naturalized or large parklike settings.

'Rehbraun' reaches 3 to 4 ft. in height and has reddish brown flower panicles that turn tan in winter. The foliage has hints of red on it in combination with glowing yellow in the autumn. It is often confused with the *Panicum virgatum* 'Hänse Herms' and 'Rotsrahlbusch' which share similar characteristics.

---

**Tracy's Notes:**

**THE PLANT**
*Perennial; sprays of reddish flowers effective July–February; foliage with hints of red and glowing yellow autumn color*

**HARDINESS**
*Zones 5–9*

**HEIGHT AND SPREAD**
*3–4 ft. × 4 ft.*

**SUN AND SHADE NEEDS**
*Sun to part shade*

**COMBINES WELL WITH**
*Black-eyed Susan, 'David' border phlox, and 'Indigo Spires' salvia*

---

*"Its form provides weight in the garden but with a light, soft, airy, almost translucent outline."*

Plants tolerate sand, clay, wet or dry soils, and are relatively salt-tolerant. The stems bend over in rainstorms or with overhead irrigation but plants stand back up when dry. They are normally upright and gorgeous over the winter but can be flattened by repeated or heavy snows. In the spring, tie string around the broad girth of the clump to contain stems and shear to the base.

*Panicum virgatum* 'Heavy Metal' and 'Prairie Sky' offer striking blue foliage while 'Shenandoah' provides the most dependable red autumn color, although it appears to be weaker-growing than other selections.

This grouping of 'Rehbraun' is decidedly ethereal when illuminated by the early morning sun.

## 'Rehbraun' switchgrass low-maintenance checklist:

✔ LONG-LIVED

✔ TOLERATES HEAT AND HUMIDITY

✔ COLD-HARDY

✔ DEER-RESISTANT

✔ INSECT AND DISEASE RESISTANT

✔ MINIMAL OR NO DEADHEADING

✔ MINIMAL OR NO FERTILIZING

✔ NO STAKING

✔ MINIMAL OR NO DIVISION

✔ MINIMAL OR NO PRUNING

✔ NON-INVASIVE

✔ DROUGHT-TOLERANT

*Panicum virgatum* 'Rehbraun' positively glows in the autumn, enhanced by reddish brown flower panicles that turn tan in winter.

## *Papaver orientale*
# Oriental poppy

**Tracy's Notes:**

THE PLANT
*Perennial; large red, orange, pink, white, violet, or salmon flowers blooming May–June; large coarse leaves*

HARDINESS
*Zones 3–7*

HEIGHT AND SPREAD
*2–3 ft. × 2 ft.*

SUN AND SHADE NEEDS
*Sun*

COMBINES WELL WITH
*Siberian iris, perennial salvia, and blue false indigo*

*"They are showstoppers in the garden and demand center stage."*

There's something magically intimate about being a close-up photographer and climbing inside the voluptuous folds of an Oriental poppy flower to experience the erotic rows of fringelike dark stamens, topped with violet anthers, encircling the swollen crowned fruit capsule. This romance is of course not reserved only for photographers, but has been shared by artists for centuries, including Georgia O'Keeffe, whose breathtaking and sensual paintings of Oriental poppies could have even the most timid of gardeners longing for such excitement in their backyards.

Because of this love affair with the flamboyant, sumptuous, Oriental poppy, I include it in this book even though, like all reputable "divas," it's not as low maintenance as most of the other plants you'll read about here. Poppies can be resilient and remain so for many years, or finicky and challenging with an ephemeral nature.

Oriental poppies come in a variety of colors, most notably fiery oranges and reds but also pinks, whites, apricots, and luscious violets (my favorite being 'Patty's Plum'). Frequently they will have intriguing violet-black blotches on the base of their petals. Due to their large size and often hot, intense color they are showstoppers in the garden and demand center stage. They are best

My favorite Oriental poppy is 'Patty's Plum', whose intriguing folds and sumptuous color are showstopping.

An up-close-and-personal view of *Papaver orientale* unveils the sheer art of its swollen crowned fruit capsule.

designed with plants that have interesting colorful foliage or later blooms that can play a subordinate role until the poppies are finished blooming. These plants can also serve to cover the hole that develops as the poppy foliage declines and disappears after flowering, returning later in the season. Individual flowers may remain for only a few days, but distinct seed capsules develop after flowering which can extend the season of interest, so don't deadhead plants.

Plants tolerate a variety of soils but resent wet overwintering conditions. They are intolerant of the humidity and heat of gardens south of zone 7.

Looking for a heart-throbbing addition to your garden? Think about the seductive Oriental poppy.

### Oriental poppy low-maintenance checklist:

LONG-LIVED

✔ TOLERATES HEAT AND HUMIDITY

✔ COLD-HARDY

✔ DEER-RESISTANT

✔ INSECT AND DISEASE RESISTANT

✔ MINIMAL OR NO DEADHEADING

✔ MINIMAL OR NO FERTILIZING

✔ NO STAKING

✔ MINIMAL OR NO DIVISION

✔ MINIMAL OR NO PRUNING

✔ NON-INVASIVE

DROUGHT-TOLERANT

# *Picea bicolor* 'Howell's Dwarf Tigertail'
# 'Howell's Dwarf Tigertail' spruce

So many dwarf and intermediate growing conifers are outstanding and low maintenance. One in particular comes to mind as being a shining star and is always valuable in designs, however, and that is *Picea bicolor* 'Howell's Dwarf Tigertail'.

'Howell's Dwarf Tigertail' spruce features needles which are green above and electrifying silver-blue on the undersides. The branches radiate outward and slightly upward in varied directions from the center of the plant creating a sculptural, wide, flat-topped form and exposing the beautiful undersurface of the needles. An incredible added bonus is the 2- to 4-in.-long erect violet cones in the spring. The cones harmonize for a monochromatic combination with *Geranium phaeum* 'Lily Lovell'

Plants work great in cool color schemes combining effectively with other blues, blue-greens, and violets such as spiny bear's breeches (*Acanthus spinosus*), 'Natalie' toadflax (*Linaria* 'Natalie'), and 'Blue Paradise' phlox (*Phlox paniculata* 'Blue Paradise'). On the other hand, they make an impressive complement to oranges such as tiger lily (*Lilium lancifolium* var. *splendens*) and 'Harvest Moon' Oriental poppy (*Papaver orientale* 'Harvest Moon'). A cool duo is 'Howell's Dwarf Tigertail' spruce with the

## Tracy's Notes:

**THE PLANT**
*Shrub; blue-green short needles; wide, flat-topped form*

**HARDINESS**
*Zone 5*

**HEIGHT AND SPREAD**
*5–6 ft. × 5–6 ft.*

**SUN AND SHADE NEEDS**
*Sun*

**COMBINES WELL WITH**
*'Lily Lovell' geranium, spiny bear's breeches, 'Natalie' toadflax, 'Blue Paradise' phlox, tiger lily, 'Harvest Moon' Oriental poppy, and 'Molly Sanderson' violet*

*"This plant is an all-around top performer that won't make you lift a finger."*

black-flowered 'Molly Sanderson' violet (*Viola* 'Molly Sanderson').

This spruce makes a remarkable specimen in a large mixed garden and works equally well in smaller condominium gardens with a touch of pruning to contain its width. It is striking in a raised container, or when used as a grouping and viewed from below in large terraced planters.

Plants are relatively slow-growing, reaching about 3 to 4 ft. high by 5 to 6 ft. wide in ten years. Ultimately they may be 5 to 6 ft. high and wide. They tolerate clay soil but are not particularly drought-resistant. Spruce in general are susceptible to a variety of pests, but by keeping the plants stress-free they should be trouble-free.

In my experience this plant is an all-around top performer that won't make you lift a finger.

### 'Howell's Dwarf Tiger' spruce low-maintenance checklist:

- ✔ LONG LIVED
- ✔ TOLERATES HEAT AND HUMIDITY
- ✔ COLD-HARDY
- ✔ DEER-RESISTANT
- ✔ INSECT AND DISEASE RESISTANT
- ✔ MINIMAL OR NO DEADHEADING
- ✔ MINIMAL OR NO FERTILIZING
- ✔ NO STAKING
- ✔ MINIMAL OR NO DIVISION
- ✔ MINIMAL OR NO PRUNING
- ✔ NON-INVASIVE
  - DROUGHT-TOLERANT

Even covered with snow, the green-above and silver-blue undersides of this shrub's needles are striking and beautiful.

'Howell's Dwarf Tigertail' spruce adds pleasing texture to cool color garden schemes.

The all-around qualities of *Picea bicolor* 'Howell's Dwarf Tigertail' won't disappoint—and its cones are stunners in and of themselves.

# *Pinus densiflora* 'Oculus-draconis'
# Dragon's-eye pine

**Tracy's Notes:**

**THE PLANT**
*Shrub; yellow-banded green needles; reddish brown flaky bark*

**HARDINESS**
*Zones 3–7*

**HEIGHT AND SPREAD**
*8–10 ft. × 8–10 ft.*

**SUN AND SHADE NEEDS**
*Sun*

**COMBINES WELL WITH**
*'Lauren's Grape' poppy, 'Saphirsprudel' blue oat grass, and Bowles' golden sedge*

*"Bring out your inner child—bring dragon's-eye pine into your garden."*

This conifer blew me away when I first saw it and it never ceases to delight and fascinate me to this day. I was sloshing through mud with nurseryman Dave Dannaher, trying to hold on to his every word while he extolled the virtues of various plants in his nursery fields, when I saw *Pinus densiflora* 'Oculus-draconis' for the first time. Well, we were like two gleeful kids sharing an exciting secret—the grower reinforcing the attributes of this stunning plant to the designer who was reeling with images of how to use it in various projects and combinations.

The needles have alternating bands of green and yellow which reportedly resemble the eye of a dragon if viewed from the proper angle. A vivid imagination may be in order for such a sighting. But it is without question that this plant acts like a magnet for the eye, attracting great attention from a distance in gardens particularly in the spring and summer. And when viewed close-up in combinations, it's amazing with violet or blue flowers and foliage. Sprinkling seeds of the annual 'Lauren's Grape' poppy (*Papaver somniferum* 'Lauren's Grape') at its feet results in a fantastic contrasting color scheme. Or for a slightly more subtle combination, consider pairing it with the blue foliage of

A striking complement to dragon's-eye pine is the contrasting color of these fantastic violet 'Lauren's Grape' poppies.

'Saphirsprudel' blue oat grass (*Helictotrichon sempervirens* 'Saphirsprudel').

Dragon's-eye pine is a large shrub or small tree perfect for the mixed garden. It will reach 8 to 10 ft. in 10 years and ultimately can reach 20 ft. after about 25 years. Simply pinching out some of the new candle growth in the spring, particularly on the main branches, can keep plants to a more compact size and tends to accentuate the variegated effect.

Plants require full sun and well-draining soil and in fact perform best in dry open conditions once established. Dry soil also seems to enhance the coloring.

Bring out your inner child—bring dragon's-eye pine into your garden.

## Dragon's-eye pine low-maintenance checklist:

✔ LONG-LIVED

✔ TOLERATES HEAT AND HUMIDITY

✔ COLD-HARDY

✔ DEER-RESISTANT

✔ INSECT AND DISEASE RESISTANT

✔ MINIMAL OR NO DEADHEADING

✔ MINIMAL OR NO FERTILIZING

✔ NO STAKING

✔ MINIMAL OR NO DIVISION

✔ MINIMAL OR NO PRUNING

✔ NON-INVASIVE

DROUGHT-TOLERANT

## *Polygonatum odoratum* 'Variegatum'
# Variegated Solomon's seal

I rank this subtle beauty as my number-one shade plant. It is graceful yet tough. So tough that once it's established it will even tolerate that dreaded condition we all so often face—drum roll, please—dry shade!

Imagine something with class, elegance, and the ruggedness to stand up to tree roots. On top of that it is bestowed with new shoots that are an artist's dream; they emerge in a blend of cream, green, and red. The leaves of *Polygonatum odoratum* 'Variegatum' are soft green edged in creamy white on arching self-supportive 2-ft. to 3-ft. stems. Dainty white bell-shaped flowers dangle from the leaf axils in the spring. Happy marriages can be made between this and innumerable shade plants. For a French country touch of blue with the creamy yellow and white of *Polygonatum*, consider pairing it with 'London Grove Blue' woodland phlox (*Phlox divaricata* 'London Grove Blue') or Siberian bugloss (*Brunnera macrophylla*).

In the autumn the leaves turn a beautiful clear yellow. After several killing frosts the stems loosen from the base and fall over, and they are easily pulled off at this time making for quick cleanup. However, don't tug on the stems or you may pull plants out of the ground. Variegated Solomon's seal plants are slow to take hold,

### Tracy's Notes:

**THE PLANT**
*Perennial; white bell-shaped flowers blooming May–June; broad green and creamy white variegated leaves turn yellow in autumn*

**HARDINESS**
*Zone 3–9*

**HEIGHT AND SPREAD**
*2–3 ft. × 2 ft.*

**SUN AND SHADE NEEDS**
*Shade*

**COMBINES WELL WITH**
*'London Grove Blue' woodland phlox, Siberian bugloss, and hellebore*

*"Happy marriages can be made between this and innumerable shade plants."*

sometime requiring several years to get established, but they are long-lived once they settle in.

This plant has it "going on" with good looks, hardiness, and ease of care—qualities every shade garden can use.

### Variegated Solomon's seal low-maintenance checklist:

✔ LONG-LIVED

✔ TOLERATES HEAT AND HUMIDITY

✔ COLD-HARDY

  DEER-RESISTANT

✔ INSECT AND DISEASE RESISTANT

✔ MINIMAL OR NO DEADHEADING

✔ MINIMAL OR NO FERTILIZING

✔ NO STAKING

✔ MINIMAL OR NO DIVISION

✔ MINIMAL OR NO PRUNING

✔ NON-INVASIVE

  DROUGHT-TOLERANT

The autumn leaves of variegated Solomon's seal saturate an otherwise subdued garden with a beautiful yellow glow.

Shade—even dry shade—will not hinder the elegant, rugged *Polygonatum odoratum* 'Variegatum'.

*Rosa rugosa* 'Hansa'
# 'Hansa' rugosa rose

**Tracy's Notes:**

**THE PLANT**
*Shrub; red-violet double flowers blooming May–September; leathery dark green leaves, large red hips, bristly thorns*

**HARDINESS**
*Zones 2–7*

**HEIGHT AND SPREAD**
*4–6 ft. × 4–6 ft.*

**SUN AND SHADE NEEDS**
*Sun*

**COMBINES WELL WITH**
*Siberian iris, lavender, and foxglove*

*"Smelling the flowers of this matriarch that has graced American gardens for over a century brings to mind images of a simpler romantic time."*

When I think of a "real" rose—one that has voluptuous clove-scented flowers and large rounded red hips, one that can ignite memories and rouse emotion—I think of *Rosa rugosa* 'Hansa'. Smelling the flowers of this matriarch that has graced American gardens for over a century brings to mind images of a simpler romantic time, when rosewater adorned boudoirs and women actually had time to sit in sitting rooms.

The big shapely buds open to richly fragrant red-violet double flowers starting in late May to early June and repeating sporadically throughout the summer. The scented petals are wonderful additions to potpourri. The robust fast-growing shrubs reach 4 to 6 ft. tall and wide and add nice weight in a mixed garden, particularly effective as an anchor on the corner of a large bed. The lustrous dark green quilted leaves are beautiful through the summer but stunning in the autumn when they change to yellow-orange. At this time the red hips develop, creating a warm color combination with the golden leaves. The hips which are attractive to birds are also said to be good for rose-hip syrup (should you be so inclined!).

Plants are extremely durable, fast-growing, disease-resistant, tolerant of cold and wet cli-

'Hansa' rugosa rose's sweet buds precede voluptuous flowers.

Visiting birds will love the glossy red hips of rugosa roses, and they can also be cooked up for rose-hip syrup!

mates as well as being salt-tolerant. Japanese beetles may be the only issue for this beauty. The straight species *Rosa rugosa* has escaped cultivation in parts of northeastern U.S. along sandy shores of the ocean and may be invasive.

For other outstanding, long-flowering, and disease-resistant choices in roses check out the Pavement and Knockout series. But never forget the adaptable and superb 'Hansa' rose.

**'Hansa' rugosa rose low-maintenance checklist:**

✔ LONG-LIVED

✔ TOLERATES HEAT AND HUMIDITY

✔ COLD-HARDY

DEER-RESISTANT

INSECT AND DISEASE RESISTANT

✔ MINIMAL OR NO DEADHEADING

✔ MINIMAL OR NO FERTILIZING

✔ NO STAKING

✔ MINIMAL OR NO DIVISION

✔ MINIMAL OR NO PRUNING

✔ NON-INVASIVE

✔ DROUGHT-TOLERANT

## *Rudbeckia maxima*
# Giant coneflower

This towering architectural coneflower makes a strong vertical statement with its large, waxy, blue-green leaves and self-supporting stems that reach 5 to 6 ft. tall. After its yellow flowers fade its prominent brown seedheads persist into early winter. Birds, particularly yellow-finch, enjoy the seeds in the summer and autumn.

Giant coneflower (aka black-eyed Susan) makes a good see-through plant near the front of the border or it will still be highly visible if planted in the back. Stems will lean a bit so space is needed to accommodate this colossal perennial, or simply prune off outer stems for use in tighter spots. It's a great way to add scale to a garden of lower growing plants or I've seen it used effectively as a specimen in a large display garden of shrubs and trees. The cloud-reaching yellow flower acted like a candle flame, pulling the eye into the space, and the leaf color, form, and textural contrast to the woody plants were dramatic.

This south-central U.S. plant is native to warm, moist pine woods and plains, thrives on summer heat and humidity, and unsurprisingly also harmonizes beautifully with other native plants such as 'Sioux Blue' Indian grass (*Sorghastrum nutans* 'Sioux Blue') and Arkansas amsonia

**Tracy's Notes:**

**THE PLANT**
*Perennial; yellow-rayed coneflowers with dark brown central seedhead blooming in June; large, waxy blue-green leaves*

**HARDINESS**
*Zones 4–9*

**HEIGHT AND SPREAD**
*5–6 ft. × 2 ft.*

**SUN AND SHADE NEEDS**
*Sun*

**COMBINES WELL WITH**
*'Sioux Blue' Indian grass, Arkansas amsonia, and limber pine*

*"It's a great way to add scale to a garden of lower-growing plants."*

(*Amsonia hubrichtii*) in a border or naturalized setting.

Minimal deadleafing will keep this plant looking tidy throughout the summer. Even though some stems will fall as winter wears on and the seedheads gradually shatter, I wait until early spring to cut back this plant.

Break away from the mundane of the typical coneflower and black-eyed Susan and plant the sky-rocketing *Rudbeckia maxima*.

## Giant coneflower low-maintenance checklist:

✔ LONG-LIVED

✔ TOLERATES HEAT AND HUMIDITY

✔ COLD-HARDY

✔ DEER-RESISTANT

✔ INSECT AND DISEASE RESISTANT

✔ MINIMAL OR NO DEADHEADING

✔ MINIMAL OR NO FERTILIZING

✔ NO STAKING

✔ MINIMAL OR NO DIVISION

✔ MINIMAL OR NO PRUNING

✔ NON-INVASIVE

✔ DROUGHT-TOLERANT

Birds—and insects!—enjoy the seeds of giant coneflower all summer and autumn.

The skyrocketing profile of *Rudbeckia maxima* makes it a good see-through plant or back-of-the-border stunner.

# *Spigelia marilandica*
# Indian pink

**Tracy's Notes:**

**THE PLANT**
*Perennial; flowers scarlet outside, yellow inside, in clusters blooming in June; mid-green foliage*

**HARDINESS**
*Zones 5–9*

**HEIGHT AND SPREAD**
*1–1 ½ ft. × 1 ft.*

**SUN AND SHADE NEEDS**
*Part to full shade*

**COMBINES WELL WITH**
*Wood poppy, golden-variegated Hakone grass, and 'Ivorine' monkshood*

*"Their bright red color is enhanced and complemented by the numerous greens in the garden."*

Add some spice to your shady garden with the attention-grabbing *Spigelia marilandica*. This underused southeastern U.S. native has intense red tubular flowers with bright yellow throats in June. It's a surprising and invigorating color to see after pastel colors have dominated the shade garden most of the spring. And it performs as the warm-up act to other hot flower colors of summer on the horizon.

Plants only reach about 1 to 1 ½ ft. and are rather common looking with simple glossy oval leaves, but the striking flowers carry a punch you won't forget. Their bright red color is enhanced and complemented by the numerous greens in the garden. They grow in part to full shade but best placement is where they can receive a touch of side or backlighting by the morning sun to add dazzle and increase their visibility. Plants combine delightfully with wood poppy (*Stylophorum diphyllum*), another native, which has bright yellow flowers in early spring but will continue to flower sporadically into the summer with sufficient moisture. Indian pinks prefer moist organic soils but reportedly tolerate drier conditions as well. The plants may be slow to establish at first but, like a fine wine, improve with age.

This little charmer of the woodland floor is a perfect addition along shaded paths or the front

Visitors in June won't just pass by Indian pink: its attention-grabbing bright red tubular flowers demand attention.

of a shaded border or naturalized area where it can be seen. It's spectacular used in large drifts for even greater impact.

Plants may be difficult to locate except from specialty or native plant nurseries. Be certain to purchase them from reputable growers who propagate them themselves and don't collect from the wild.

For some zest in the early summer garden, consider the vivacious eye-catching Indian pink.

### Indian pink low-maintenance checklist:

✔ LONG-LIVED

✔ TOLERATES HEAT AND HUMIDITY

✔ COLD-HARDY

✔ DEER-RESISTANT

✔ INSECT AND DISEASE RESISTANT

✔ MINIMAL OR NO DEADHEADING

✔ MINIMAL OR NO FERTILIZING

✔ NO STAKING

✔ MINIMAL OR NO DIVISION

✔ MINIMAL OR NO PRUNING

✔ NON-INVASIVE

DROUGHT-TOLERANT

## *Syneilesis aconitifolia*
# Shredded umbrella plant

One wonders how exciting a plant could be with a common name like shredded umbrella plant. It ranks right up there with lungwort, deadnettle, stinking hellebore, and bull's blood beet. Honestly, what marketing genius comes up with these goofy names for such great plants?

*Syneilesis aconitifolia* sits unassumingly on the edge of a path in a shady part of my garden. Although it's not an in-your-face extrovert, it is subtly dynamic. It's rarely seen growing in gardens but it's one of the plants visitors to my garden ask about the most.`

In the spring this northeast Asian native emerges with white woolly leaves in the fashion of our native May apple (*Podophyllum peltatum*). The fascinating and unusual leaves are serrated and deeply cut and yes, umbrella shaped, with drooping fingerlike lobes. They resemble the leaves of the fernleaf fullmoon maple (*Acer japonicum* 'Aconitifolium'), and both plants share a similar name meaning aconitum leaved (aconitum, or monkhood, a herbaceous perennial, has somewhat comparable leaves, hence the namesake).

*Syneilesis aconitifolia* leaves become less hairy with age, broadening to about 12 in., and are held atop 18-in. narrow stems. They create a finely cut and distinct texture.

### Tracy's Notes:

**THE PLANT**
*Perennial; serrated, deeply cut, umbrella-shaped woolly leaves with drooping fingerlike lobes; rather insignificant small pinkish white flowers blooming July–September*

**HARDINESS**
*Zones 5–8*

**HEIGHT AND SPREAD**
*18–24 in. × 10–12 in.*

**SUN AND SHADE NEEDS**
*Part shade to sun*

**COMBINES WELL WITH**
*'Brilliance' autumn fern, purple burnet, and variegated Solomon's seal*

*"It's rarely seen growing in gardens but it's one of the plants visitors to my garden ask about the most."*

Underwhelming daisylike sprays of pinkish white flowers are borne in the summer on tall stems above the foliage. I find them distracting from the true show and often opt to prune them off. Clumps are slow to increase, eventually reaching about 2 ft. in width after six to seven years. Plants prefer moist shade but tolerate drier conditions once established.

Once you see this unusual plant you'll be thinking with excitement "shredded umbrellas all around"!

### Shredded umbrella plant low-maintenance checklist:

✔ LONG-LIVED

✔ TOLERATES HEAT AND HUMIDITY

✔ COLD-HARDY

✔ DEER-RESISTANT

✔ INSECT AND DISEASE RESISTANT

✔ MINIMAL OR NO DEADHEADING

✔ MINIMAL OR NO FERTILIZING

✔ NO STAKING

✔ MINIMAL OR NO DIVISION

✔ MINIMAL OR NO PRUNING

✔ NON-INVASIVE

DROUGHT-TOLERANT

Shredded umbrella plant emerges in spring with white woolly leaves that look positively prehistoric.

Like its unlikely common name, shredded umbrella plant, *Syneilesis aconitifolia* adds the unexpected with its unusual leaves with drooping finger-like lobes.

# *Thalictrum* 'Elin'
# 'Elin' meadow rue

**Tracy's Notes:**

**THE PLANT**
*Perennial; lavender and pale yellow flower clusters blooming late June–August; smoky purple deeply cut foliage fading to blue-green*

**HARDINESS**
*Zones 3–7*

**HEIGHT AND SPREAD**
*6–8 ft. × 3 ½ ft.*

**SUN AND SHADE NEEDS**
*Sun to part shade*

**COMBINES WELL WITH**
*Dwarf Rocky Mountain fir, Japanese white pine, and 'Ogon' dawn redwood*

*"The lavender and pale yellow flower clusters form puffy clouds that float high over the heads of most other plants."*

This lofty 8-ft. meadow rue is just starting to make its way into the hearts of gardeners. I was blown away the first spring *Thalictrum* 'Elin' emerged in my garden sporting magnificent new purple shoots that unfurled into a mound of smoky purple deeply cut foliage. The new leaves hold this color longer than on other meadow rues, not fading until around mid-June and then to an also-lovely blue-green. The lavender and pale yellow flower clusters form puffy clouds that float high over the heads of most other plants. Stately self-supportive purple-infused stems carry the show.

This plant received a four-star rating from the Chicago Botanic Garden's plant evaluation of meadow rue in 2007, and researcher Richard Hawke noted that it exhibited great vigor, yet maintained a dense, bushy habit through the summer, and did not drop leaves like some of its relatives ('Elin' is a hybrid between *Thalictrum rochebruneanum* and *T. flavum* subsp. *glaucum*). It was also highly rated for flower production, blooming from late June to mid-August, as well as winter hardiness and overall good plant health. In only two of the study's six years (conducted 1998 through 2003) was powdery mildew a problem and plants also had slight leaf miner damage most years but not enough to impair their ornamental qualities.

The smoky purple foliage of 'Elin' meadow rue holds its color until fading in mid-June to an also-lovely blue-green.

Puffy clouds of *Thalictrum* 'Elin' are stately, floating high above the heads of the other plants.

Plants in these studies were grown in approximately ten hours of sun a day and exposed to wind—it is Chicago after all. The maintenance was minor to simulate average home garden conditions (no offense taken) and plants were watered as needed but did not receive any fertilization, routine cutting back, or winter protection.

I'm sold, aren't you?

### 'Elin' meadow rue low-maintenance checklist:

- ✔ LONG-LIVED
- ✔ TOLERATES HEAT AND HUMIDITY
- ✔ COLD-HARDY
- ✔ DEER-RESISTANT
- ✔ INSECT AND DISEASE RESISTANT
- ✔ MINIMAL OR NO DEADHEADING
- ✔ MINIMAL OR NO FERTILIZING
- ✔ NO STAKING
- ✔ MINIMAL OR NO DIVISION
- ✔ MINIMAL OR NO PRUNING
- ✔ NON-INVASIVE
- DROUGHT-TOLERANT

## *Yucca filamentosa* 'Color Guard'
# 'Color Guard' yucca

Do you, like me, long for strong architectural form and striking leaf color such as found on variegated *Agave* and *Furcraea* but in a plant hardy for gardens further north? A plant that would be effective in the garden all year rather than being condemned to the great indoors for the winter? Then *Yucca filamentosa* 'Color Guard' is your answer. A yucca, you say? Well this isn't the "yucky yucca" that you may remember adorning cemeteries or old landscapes which required a backhoe to remove.

This is a pulse-quickening plant with broad, sword-shaped leaves sporting a cream to bright yellow stripe up the center of each leaf with leaf margins edged in variable stripes of green. The margins also have curious fine curly white hairs or filaments and may be suffused with pink in the autumn or winter. The leaves are nothing short of brilliant when backlit. And they look amazing in countless combinations in the garden all year particularly adding some punch to the winter garden, when the depth of the leaf color intensifies. They glow like luminaries against the snow. 'Color Guard' yucca is stunning in combination with winter-flowering plants such as the witchhazels (cultivars of *Hamamelis* ×*intermedia*). For an artistic complement, combine them with 'Hoopsii' blue spruce (*Picea pungens* 'Hoopsii').

### Tracy's Notes:

**THE PLANT**
*Shrub; yellow-centered leaves turn pink and coral in winter; masses of creamy white flowers on large spikes blooming in July–August*

**HARDINESS**
*Zones 4–9*

**HEIGHT AND SPREAD**
*2–3 ft. × 2 ft.*

**SUN AND SHADE NEEDS**
*Sun*

**COMBINES WELL WITH**
*Witchhazels, 'Hoopsii' blue spruce, and 'Ogon' spirea*

*"The leaves are nothing short of brilliant when backlit."*

Plants age gracefully to slowly form clumps with multiple rosettes. Tall 3- to 5-ft. spikes emerge from the center of the plant carrying bell-shaped white flowers in the summer.

You won't find a much tougher plant tolerating northern conditions, wind, heat, humidity, poor soil, part shade, and drought once established. It is best to avoid wet soils, however.

Striking color, texture, and form make this yucca the hardy agave-like choice for colder regions.

## 'Color Guard' yucca low-maintenance checklist:

✔ LONG-LIVED

✔ TOLERATES HEAT AND HUMIDITY

✔ COLD-HARDY

✔ DEER-RESISTANT

✔ INSECT AND DISEASE RESISTANT

✔ MINIMAL OR NO DEADHEADING

✔ MINIMAL OR NO FERTILIZING

✔ NO STAKING

✔ MINIMAL OR NO DIVISION

✔ MINIMAL OR NO PRUNING

✔ NON-INVASIVE

✔ DROUGHT-TOLERANT

The luminescent glow of 'Color Guard' yucca combines impressively with the golden sunlit foliage of 'Ogon' spirea.

The sword-shaped, bright-yellow-striped leaves of *Yucca filamentosa* 'Color Guard' are not just striking, they are incredibly low-care and effective year round.

# Sources

The following list is just a small selection of the many nurseries around the country which may carry the plants featured in this book.

Acorn Farms
7679 Worthington Road
Galena, OH 43021
614.891.9348
www.acornfarms.com

André Viette Farm and Nursery
994 Long Meadow Road
Fisherville, VA 22939
1.800.575.5538
www.viette.com

Baker's Acres Greenhouse
3388 Castle Road
Alexandria, OH 43001
1.800.934.6525
www.bakersacresgreenhouse.com

Beds and Borders, Inc.
P.O. Box 616
600 Laurel Lane
Laurel, NY 11948
631.298.1836
www.bedsandborders.com

Behnke Nurseries
11300 Baltimore Avenue
Beltsville MD, 20705
301.937.1100
www.behnkes.com

Blanchette Gardens
267 Rutland Street
Carlisle, MA 01741
978.369.2962
www.blanchettegardens.com

Blooms Nursery Online
383 Coal Hill Road
Clearfield, PA 16830
814.765.0153
www.bloomsnurserypa.com

Bordine Nursery, Ltd.
8600 Dixie Highway
Clarkston, MI 48348-4236
248.625.9100
www.bordines.com

Brent and Becky's Bulbs
7900 Daffodil Lane
Gloucester, VA 23061
877.661.2852
www.BrentandBeckysBulbs.com

Brotzman's Nursery
6899 Chapel Road
Madison, OH 44057
440.428.3361
www.brotzmansnursery.com

Carroll Gardens
444 E. Main Street
Westminster, MD 21157
800.638.6334
www.carrollgardens.com

Cistus Nursery
22711 NW Gillihan Road
Sauvie Island, OR 97231
503.621.2233
www.cistus.com

Collector's Nursery
16804 NE 102nd Avenue
Battle Ground, WA 98604
360.574.3832
www.collectorsnursery.com

Creek Hill Nursery
17 W. Main Street
Leola, PA 17540
717.556.0000
www.creekhillnursery.com

Dannaher Landscaping, Inc.
12200 Vans Valley Road
Galena, OH 43021
740.965.3789
www.dannaherlandscaping.com

Digging Dog Nursery
P.O. Box 471
Albion, CA 95410
707.937.1130
www.diggingdog.com

Fairweather Gardens
P.O. Box 330
Greenwich, NJ 08323
856.451.6261
www.fairweathergardens.com

Forestfarm Nursery
990 Tetherow Road
Williams, OR 97544-9599
541.846.7269
www.forestfarm.com

Gardens on the Prairie
3242 W. 169th Avenue
Lowell, IN 46356
219.690.0911
www.gardensontheprairie.com

Geraniaceae
122 Hilcrest Avenue
Kentfield, CA 94904
415.461.4168
www.geraniaceae.com

Glasshouse Works
P.O. Box 97
Church Street
Stewart, OH 45778
740.662.2142
www.glasshouseworks.com

Gossler Farms Nursery
1200 Weaver Road
Springfield, OR 97478-9691
541.746.3922
www.gosslerfarms.com

Herman Losely and Son
3410 Shepard Road
Perry, OH 44081
440.259.2725
www.losely.com

Homewood Farm
19520 Nunda Road
Howard, OH 43028
740.599.6638

Joy Creek Nursery
20300 NW Watson Road
Scappoose, OR 97056
503.543.7474
www.joycreek.com

Klehm's Song Sparrow
Perennial Farm
13101 E. Rye Road
Avalon, WI 53505
1.800.553.3715
www.songsparrow.com

Klyn Nurseries, Inc.
3322 S. Ridge Road
P.O. Box 343
Perry, OH 44081
1.800.860.8104
www.klynnurseries.com

Kurt Bluemel, Inc.
2740 Greene Lane
Baldwin, MD 21013
1.800.498.1560
www.kurtbluemel.com

Lake County Nursery
P.O. Box 122
State Route 84
Perry, OH 44081
1.800.522.5253
www.lakecountynursery.com

Landcraft Environments
1160 E. Mill Road
Mattituck, NY 11952-1289
631.298.3510
www.landcraftenvironment.com

Millcreek Gardens
15088 Smart-Cole Road
Ostrander, OH 43061
1.800.948.1234
www.millcreekgardensohio.com

Mountain Laurel Nursery
906 Round Bottom Road
Milford, OH 45245
513.831.5800

Niche Gardens
1111 Dawson Road
Chapel Hill, NC 27516
919.967.0078
www.nichegardens.com

North Creek Nursery
388 North Creek Road
Landenberg, PA 19350
1.877.326.7584
www.northcreeknurseries.com

Plant Delights Nursery
9241 Sauls Road
Raleigh, NC 27603
919.772.4794
www.plantdelights.com

The Planter's Palette
28 W. 571 Roosevelt Road
Winfield, IL 60190
630.293.1040
www.planterspalette.com

Seely's Landscape Nursery
3265 Walcutt Road
Hilliard, OH 43026
614.876.1838
www.seelyslandscape.com

Singing Springs Nursery
8802 Wilkerson Road
Cedar Grove, NC 27231
919.732.9403

Siskiyou Rare Plant Nursery
2115 Talent Avenue
Talent, OR 97540
541.535.7103
www.srpn.net

Sunny Border
3637 State Route 167
Jefferson, OH 44047
1.800.577.1760
www.sunnyborderohio.com

Sunshine Farms and Gardens
HC 67, Box 539B
Renick, WV 24966
304.497.2208
www.sunfarm.com

Tranquil Lake Nursery
45 River Street
Rehoboth, MA 02769
508.252.4002
www.tranquil-lake.com

Wade and Gatton Nursery
1288 Gatton Rocks Road
Bellville, OH 44813
419.886.2094

Walters Gardens
P.O. Box 137
1992 96th Avenue
Zeeland, MI 49464
1.888.925.8377
www.waltersgardens.com

Waterloo Gardens
200 N. Whitford Road
Exton, PA 19341-2099
610.363.0800
www.waterloogardens.com

Wayside Gardens
1 Garden Lane
Hodges, SC 29695
800.213.0379
www.waysidegardens.com

Woodside Gardens
1191 Egg and I Road
Chimacum, WA 98325
1.800.732.4754

Yucca Do Nursery
P.O. Box 104
Hempstead, TX 77445
979.826.4580
www.yuccado.com

# Additional reading

Armitage, Allan M. *Herbaceous Perennial Plants: A Treatise on their Identification, Culture, and Garden Attributes.* Second Edition. Champaign: Stipes Publishing, 1998.

Burrell, C. Colston and Judith Knott Tyler. *Hellebores: A Comprehensive Guide.* Portland: Timber Press, 2006.

Darke, Rick. *The Encyclopedia of Grasses for Livable Landscapes.* Portland: Timber Press, 2006.

Dirr, Michael A. *Manual of Woody Landscape Plants: Their Identification, Ornamental Characteristics, Culture, Propagation and Uses.* Fifth Edition. Champaign: Stipes Publishing, 1998.

DiSabato-Aust, Tracy. *The Well-Designed Mixed Garden: Building Beds and Borders with Trees, Shrubs, Perennials, Annuals and Bulbs.* Portland: Timber Press, 2003.

——. *The Well-Tended Perennial Garden: Planting and Pruning Techniques.* Portland: Timber Press, 2006.

Rice, Graham, and Kurt Bluemel. *Encyclopedia of Perennials: The Definitive Illustrated Reference Guide* (American Horticultural Society). New York: DK Publishing, 2006.

# Photography credits

Adrian Bloom, 30, 63, 99, 117, 126, back cover (right)

Richard Bloom, cover (middle right, right), 15, 18, 24, 27, 33, 39, 51, 54, 55, 75, 84, 90, 91, 97, 111, 150, 153

Jonathan Buckley, 36

Tracy DiSabato-Aust, cover (left, middle left), 2, 5, 6, 7, 8, 11, 16, 19, 21, 22, 25, 28, 31, 34, 37, 40, 43, 46, 48, 49, 52, 55, 57, 58, 61, 64, 67, 69, 70, 72, 73, 76, 78, 79, 82, 85, 87, 88, 91, 93, 94, 96, 102, 103, 105, 106, 109, 112, 115, 118, 121, 124, 127, 130, 132, 133, 136, 138, 139, 141, 142, 144, 145, 148, 151, 154, 157, 160, 163, back cover (left, middle right)

Carole Drake, 45

Deb Goff, back cover (author)

Marcus Harpur, 123

Saxon Holt, 129

Dianna Jazwinski, 135, 159, back cover (middle left)

Andrea Jones, 60

Todd Meier/*Fine Gardening*, 42

Graham Rice/GardenPhotos.com, 120, 156, 162

Virginia Small/*Fine Gardening*, cover (author)

Graham Strong, 66, 114

Visions, 81

judywhite/GardenPhotos.com, 108, 147